Eighteen Sermons
and
Two *Divrei Torah*

Rabbi Yaakov ben Avrohom

Riverdale Electronic Books
Dublin, Ohio

Eighteen Sermons
and
Two *Divrei Torah*

Rabbi Yaakov ben Avrohom

Riverdale Electronic Books
Dublin, Ohio

Eighteen Sermons and Two *Divrei Torah*
© 1993, 2011, Rabbi Yaakov ben Avrohom. All rights reserved.

No part of this book may be reproduced or transmitted in any form or by any means, graphic, electronic, or mechanical, including but not limited to photocopying, recording, taping, or by any information storage retrieval system, without permission in writing from the publisher.

Riverdale Electronic Books
Dublin, Ohio
http://RiverdaleeBooks.com

The opinions expressed in this collection are the author's, and do not necessarily reflect those of C.E.B. Pubs, Riverdale Electronic Books, or their officers, employees, or agents, or of any wholesaler or retailer that may be involved in the distribution of this work.

ISBN: 978-1-932606-32-4

Published by special arrangement with C.E.B. Pubs.

Published in the United States of America

Contents

Introduction	vii
Being Religious	1
Gittin and Answerability	5
Shifting the Blame	11
D'var Torah: Acharei Mos/Kedoshim	17
Cults	21
Do You Believe in God?	26
End of Days	31
A Sense of Compulsion	36
Reacting to Others	41
Programming	46
Abortion and Suicide	51
D'var Torah: Shoftim	56
Shoot the Doctor	60
Content or *Kavanah*	65
Jewish Thinking	68
First Evening Rosh Ha'Shanah	72
First Morning Rosh Ha'Shanah	78
Second Evening Rosh Ha'Shanah	83
Second Morning Rosh Ha'Shanah	88
Thinking Jewish	93

Introduction

The sermons in this volume are in essentially chronological order, and were delivered in 1993. The date is important, for it provides a context. During that period we worried about cults, both ordinary and Satanic, but didn't worry about Islamic expansionism. Or, perhaps more correctly, we didn't worry that much about Islamic expansionism outside of Islam's traditional borders. The Gulf War had been over for three years, and had only involved one Arab country invading another. No great threat was seen to our own country. Certainly, it was not generally recognized that anyone was still taking the Koranic directive for world conquest seriously.

In 1993, we still thought that civilization had arrived even in the Islamic world. We know better now. It's curious that a strict adherence to what is believed to be God's law, which we find meritorious in Judaism, is capable of producing so much trouble for the world with Moslems. Perhaps the real contrast is that Jews, even very early in our history, were always looking for lenient interpretations of Law, while Moslems seem to prefer the strictest. We look at "an eye for an eye" as a demand for equivalent monetary compensation, while the Moslem is more likely to take it literally. So do a lot of Christians, though mostly so they can argue that our

God is this strict, cruel deity, and theirs is much nicer and more compassionate (though somehow they tend to miss that this argument sort of undermines their contention it's the same God). Likewise, Jewish law specifies death by stoning for adultery, but then imposes a standard of evidence in such cases that makes conviction — much less execution — virtually impossible. Islamic regimes seem to take an inordinate delight in killing women.

For all practical purposes this sort of thing isn't even touched upon in any of these sermons. The notion of Islam being a real threat was still seen as a relic of the Middle Ages.

These sermons were written for, and delivered to, a Jewish congregation. Specifically, a Conservative Jewish congregation with traditionalist leanings. We had mixed seating — though the sanctuary had been designed to provide for separation of the sexes when it was built in the 1920s — and the majority of the members drove to *shul* on *shabbos*, and probably drove elsewhere as well. I walked, and was one of the few who did. I ate a lot of hot dogs, for it was a 50 mile drive to the nearest kosher market, and in the local community "kosher" was pretty much limited to Hebrew National products at the Giant Eagle. The local Jewish community had once supported kosher butchers and markets, but over the years most of the young people had moved away and the congregation now consisted mainly of people in their late 50s and up. Not enough to support that sort of infrastructure.

It isn't always easy to get people to listen when the rabbi is the same age or younger than the majority of the members' children. You still try, though.

Most of these sermons were delivered on *erev shabbos*. The *divrei Torah*, obviously, are from *shabbos* mornings.

One or two were also written for the Tuesday evening *minyan*, which was usually preceded by a short lesson. And Rosh Ha'Shanah 5754 is well covered in this volume.

I must admit, I wasn't always the most popular rabbi who ever lived when I delivered some of these. It is a rabbi's job to shake up his congregation, to make them uncomfortable with where they are and inspire them to become greater. Naturally, not everyone likes to be reminded that he isn't doing as much as he could. In general, my sermons were most popular when they just taught a general lesson, or reported on something from current events. When I found myself compelled to push greater observance, or make suggestions that might benefit the community but inconvenience some of the members—such as suggesting working to bring more jobs to town so that their children would be more likely to remain a part of the community—I could expect to hear from the "experts" on why that wasn't practical. I was also sometimes taken to task for being unfamiliar with some specific nuance of ritual—which always turned out to be some local *minhag* you would only know about if you were born in that town, but they believed was common everywhere.

It has been said that if a rabbi (or, for that matter, a priest or minister) is *too* popular, he probably isn't doing his job.

Given the intended audience for the sermons and *div'rei Torah* contained in this little volume, the reader should probably not be too surprised if Christian beliefs are referred to as mythology. If a Jew believed those stories to be true, he wouldn't be a Jew. For that matter, if they actually *were* true, we would have listened when their candidate was still alive.

The transliterations of Hebrew words and phrases

in these sermons and *divrei Torah* follow the Ashkenazic pronunciation pattern, which was employed by most members of the congregation where they were delivered. This may sound a little funny to many younger Jews, who have been raised with the so-called Sephardic pronunciation employed in modern Israeli Hebrew. What's in this book follows the rule that, at least in prayer, a Jew is to pronounce Hebrew according to his own tradition.

Given that Israeli Hebrew pronunciation was originally intended to separate the daily Hebrew language from the language of the liturgy, and is really neither Ashkenazic nor Sephardic, but a strange combination of the two, I feel justified in keeping the traditional form here.

Being Religious

[April 16, 1993] When I was in Florida, there was a particular congregant who used to constantly confuse me. There was one thing he was adamant about—he was *not* religious. I don't know how many times he told me that, but he made sure that I knew it.

Okay—fine—he wasn't religious. We all know people who aren't. What was confusing about this, though, was that, except when he was out of town, I don't remember him ever missing a service. I had several congregants who claimed that they *were* religious, yet I'd see them only on festivals. This man, who was definitely *not* religious, was there every week.

I think this whole concept of "being religious" is one Jews have a problem with. Often, we're not even sure of how to define it. Is being religious a way of feeling? A form of belief? A scrupulous adherence to a particular set of behavioral patterns? Being a member of a synagogue? Giving to identifiably Jewish charities?

It is all of these? Or none of these?

My old friend, who never missed a service, but wasn't religious, was a member of a synagogue. He attended services. By these standard, most would call him religious.

Part of the confusion comes from the tendency to

confuse "religious" with "Orthodox." They're not the same. There are non-Orthodox Jews who are thoroughly religious, and there are Orthodox Jews who have never had the least twinge of a religious feeling.

You might say that we sometimes confuse the means with the end. What is the point of observance? Why do we make a special point of diet? Why do we consider it wrong to handle money on *shabbos*?

We can do all of these things, keep a kosher home, be strictly *shomer shabbos*, keep our heads covered at all times, and so on. Yet this doesn't necessarily make us better people. The book of *Isaiah*, after all, begins with a lecture on the futility of sacrifices that are not accompanied by a real change in the person who brings them. In the same way, observance lacks any real meaning unless it also results in a better person.

Why do we have rules? We have them because we recognize that people, left to their own devices, will usually do whatever is most beneficial to themselves, and the rest of the world can go hang. We outlaw robbery not in order to deter those who are truly lacking in moral restraint, but to deter the ordinary people who might be tempted and, lacking any commonly-held opinion to the contrary, could give in to that temptation. The thieves are going to rob because that's what they do. The good people do not, at least in part, because the standards of their culture say it's wrong.

It's like putting a padlock on the tool shed. It won't keep out a determined thief, but it will keep your neighbor from "borrowing" your hedge clippers without telling you.

In much the same way, observance is intended to lead to the right mental attitudes. What is religion, after all, but a way of relating the God? Judaism is defined as a covenantal relationship. In return for our obedience to his laws, God promises to do certain things for us. That these things have not yet happened may be blamed, say our prophets, on the fact that we haven't completely lived up to our end of the bargain.

Martin Buber called relationships central. But he also warned that, for too many of us, the relationship is wrong. We relate to God in an "I–It" manner. We, the "I," are real, but our creator is reduced to an object. An "It." True, this constitutes a start. "I–It" is clearly better than "I–Nothing." But it can never be more than an intermediate level.

If God is an "It," he is less real than the "I." An "It" is something to be manipulated. Children think of God as an "It." Children, when they pray, mostly ask for things for themselves. They say, "bless Mommy and Daddy" because they know Mommy and Daddy are listening, but the real sincerity is reserved for the "…and please bring me a new bicycle."

The earliest concepts of religion were based on assigning a divine character to natural phenomena, and then trying to manipulate these "gods" through prayer and ritual. As humanity became more sophisticated, the number of gods decreased, and the concept of the divine became less subject to human manipulation.

Yet, so long as we look at our relationship with God as "I–It," we haven't quite got beyond that most basic level.

Buber taught that what was really needed was an "I–Thou" relationship. Since Buber wrote in German, he actually said *"Ich–Du,"* a phrase that no longer translates very well into modern English. Today, when we say "thou," we tend to think we're speaking very formally. In fact, "thou" is the intimate form of "you." It's how you might speak to a parent, or your child, your lover, or your closest friend.

"Thou" isn't something you'd call your boss, or a stranger. It implies a degree of closeness transcending the casual. Someone in a position of authority would be addressed as "you," which is actually the formal form of address in English. We would use "thou" as a form of address to a superior only to a monarch, or to God, because both a considered as standing in the position of a parent to their subjects.

And this is the point of religion. To bring the individual into an intimate relationship with his or her creator. It isn't to insure that we stand in a particular posture when we say *Aleinu*, or to demand that we drink no less than 3.3 ounces of wine from each of the four cups at the *seder*. The little details of ritual and observance are intended to allow us to concentrate on the *kavanah*, and are not and end in themselves.

When we speak to the Divine, we cannot think of him as an object to be manipulated for our own good. We stand in a covenantal relationship. Each has the obligation to do certain things for the other, as long as both sides keep the bargain. Since God is the creator, and we are the created, we tend to make the mistakes. Our religion teaches us how to avoid these errors. How to relate to God, and to our fellow human beings.

Which is what religion is all about.

Gittin and Answerability

[April 23, 1993] How many of you watched *L.A. Law* last night? It was a very interesting show, because it pointed up a particular problem in today's Jewish community. The plot of this particular story line was relatively simple. A Jewish couple was divorcing, and the wife asked for a *get*.

The husband's first response was entirely too typical of many Jews today. He wanted to know, "What's a *get?*" Since the Reform movement abandoned the whole idea of a Jewish divorce document decades ago, arguing that the civil divorce also meets the Torah requirements, the issue generally doesn't come up in their families. And, even more to the point, many Jews today simply don't receive an adequate Jewish education. Many, like the character in the show, are simply unaware that Jewish law requires a separate document to end a marriage.

Once he finds out what's involved, however, the husband's initial willingness to go along turns into the sort of behavior that has become typical in recent years. He'll give the *get*, but only if his wife lets him keep the house, leaves his business shares alone, and so on. Since the husband has to give the *get* of his own free will, and the wife has to receive it in the same way, either one can arbitrarily put a stop to the whole procedure.

In reality, though, the husband has all the power. If the wife refuses to accept a *get*, her husband can still remarry. The civil divorce frees him from state and federal bigamy laws, and Jewish law has never actually limited a man to a single wife. Only a decree of Rabbeinu Gershom makes monogamy mandatory for Ashkenazic Jews. A decree, by the way, that expires in another seven years [2000 CE].

The wife, however, cannot simply remarry without a *get*. No Conservative or Orthodox rabbi would ever agree to officiate at the remarriage of a divorced woman unless she can produce a valid *get*. After all, if she remarries without one, any children born of the second marriage are *mamzerim*, and that creates a whole new set of problems.

Now, *L.A. Law* is obviously fiction. But the problem is a very real one. Many husbands have made extortionate demands before agreeing to a *get*. It's not at all unusual for child custody to be given to the father not because he would be a better parent, but because this was the only condition under which he would allow his ex-wife to remarry. Even more frequent are demands for money.

The publisher of a major Jewish newspaper has carried on a long-running campaign to make life miserable for his son-in-law, because the son-in-law has consistently refused to provide a *get* without being paid an exorbitant sum.

The TV show solved the problem in a typical TV way. While the negotiations continue, and the husband argues that if she wants the *get*, his wife will have to give him whatever he wants, because he holds all the cards and, anyway, God doesn't go in for direct punishment any more, the TV news comes on and informs them all that there's been a mud slide. Alone along the entire coast road, *his* house was just washed into the Pacific.

Don't you just love accountability.

From a philosophical viewpoint, *L.A. Law* was taking what might be called a covenantal outlook. This is the oldest of all ideas as to how humanity in general, and Jews in particular, relate to God. There is a covenant, a contract, drawn up between the Almighty and us. Since God has all the power, he gets to set the rules.

Historians have pointed out that the covenants established with Adam and Chava, with Noach, and with Abraham, all bear a strong resemblance to the suzerainty agreements between Canaanite kings and their vassals. The one with the real power is the one who sets the rules of behavior, and in return for obedience agrees to provide certain specific benefits. These agreements also provide a set of fairly horrible punishments for disobedience.

One of the unique characteristics of the Jewish covenantal pacts is the degree of accountability placed upon us. The full responsibility for obedience is placed on our own shoulders. Unlike other cultures, we are bound to a strict monotheism that precludes the very possibility of a devil or other evil influence affecting our behavior. If there really was a devil, after all, how could we be held accountable for our actions? We'd always have someone else to blame.

There is an ancient Talmudic dictim that declares that God loves to be talked out of his harsh decrees. We find this demonstrated just after the incident of the Golden Calf, when God tells Moses that he is going to kill every Israelite and start the whole thing over with Moses and his family. Moses argues, successfully, that this would be bad public relations. He points out that the Egyptians would certainly ridicule a God who went to all that trouble to free his people, only to kill them all a few months later. Perhaps the earliest example of someone asking, "What would the *goyim* think?"

Yet, at other times, the decree remained in effect. In the 8th century BCE, the northern tribes had slid so far into the worship of alien gods that Assyria was given power over them, and they vanished into an exile from which they have never returned.

In the 6th century BCE, Judah was conquered and sent into exile in Babylon for the same reasons. The difference, this time, was that we were able to preserve our faith even in exile, and at the end of 70 years were allowed to return home and rebuild the Temple.

This was the standard. A sort of cause-and-effect concept of religion and morality. The sages taught that death came into the world because Adam was unable to obey a simple command not to eat a particular fruit. They taught, in fact, that death itself was always a punishment for sin — though in most cases the sin was a minor one, and the period between the sin and the execution might be many years.

Even Moses was condemned to die across the Jordan from *Eretz Yisroel* for something seemingly as minor as losing his temper for an instant and hitting a rock with his staff, instead of just speaking to it. Since the true meaning of "sin" is "to fall short," there are none of us who can avoid it.

Sin is an inevitable consequence of free will. If we have the ability to choose between good and evil, then we will inevitably sometimes chose wrong. No death without sin, the Rabbis said. And, conversely, no life either, for we cannot live without making mistakes. We can only do our best to see that the mistakes are minor, and that the punishment should be delayed as long as possible.

Cause and effect. That's the root of covenant theology. Yet, as *Job* teaches, we lack the all-encompassing vision to make the connections. Just as the flapping of a butterfly's wings in Tokyo may eventually cause a hurricane in the south Atlantic, so may an unkind word 30 years ago be the ultimate cause of death early in the next century.

We're uncomfortable with this sort of thinking today. The American Legion magazine I receive today devoted quite a bit of space to an interview with an author who argues that our modern philosophy has eliminated guilt. That there are only victims, no villains. That we treat anti-social behavior as some sort of disease, and not as a simple decision to ignore the rules. We think that if anything bad happens to us, we can't possibly be at fault. It's always someone else's fault.

Well, as much as we hate to do it, sometimes we have to admit that it's *not* someone else's fault. That, somewhere along the line, we did something to deserve this. Or, perhaps, one of our ancestor did something to deserve this, as God himself has declared that he would punish a sinner unto the fourth generation. We often complain that the innocent sometimes suffer along with the guilty—or even in place of the guilty—yet the Torah warns us that this will happen. Our actions affect not only ourselves, but our descendants as well.

And, most of the time, we're not going to be presented with a clear-cut cause-and-effect punishment, like the one on *L.A. Law*. Most of the time we're going to be presented with many more questions than answers. Why do bad things happen to good people? I don't know. Rabbi Kerschner didn't know either, but we all have to admit they happen.

Our only option, really, is to try to live our own lives in the way the Torah teaches, and to always try to make the right decisions.

The results, really, are up to us.

Shifting the Blame

[April 30, 1993] I'm really beginning to like what they've done with *L.A. Law*. Not only has the show improved dramatically in the last few weeks, but, for the second straight week, the writers have been kind enough to give me the starting point for a sermon.

One of the cases they argued on last night's show involved the great-granddaughter of a slave, suing the great-grandson of his owner over paintings he'd done while he was a slave. The case provided a nice contrast between perceptions of justice and of law. After listening to all the arguments—the primary argument being that a slave could not freely give his work to his master because, as a slave, he entirely lacked any freedom of choice in the matter—the jury decided in favor of the plaintiff. They didn't give her the paintings, but they awarded her the value.

That's where we find the perception of justice.

The law came in a moment later, when the judge did something judges are allowed to do, but usually don't. In effect, he said, "Well, I'm sure the verdict feels right, but you're thinking emotionally, and this is really a question of law, and the law doesn't support the verdict." So he threw out the verdict and dismissed the case.

He ruled that questions of consent were irrelevant.

Since slavery was legal at the time the paintings were done, there had been a legal transfer of title. Our modern opinions on the subject didn't matter. To uphold the jury's verdict would have meant punishing the great-grandson for the actions of his ancestor.

Now, what does this have to do with Judaism? Jewish law is very specific in this area. The only person who can be held responsible for a crime, or for a sin, is the person who actually committed it. The Torah declares that we may never punish the parent for the crimes of the child, nor may we punish the child for the crimes of the parent. Each is to be held responsible for his own actions.

We might contrast this with the current trend toward laws that make a parent responsible for the criminal actions of their children. The modern sociological sense of justice, which assumes that every action is motivated by outside causes, and that no one ever does anything simply because they felt like doing it, is codified in these laws. Since the children who commit crimes can't be responsible for their own actions, their parents have to be. That's the logic.

It's similar to a case a few years ago in which a man successfully sued the Colt Firearms company because the safety catch on a 60-year-old gun broke and he managed to shot himself in the foot. The man actually won. Only a few years earlier the case would probably have been laughed right out of court. The defense would have argued—correctly, I think —that only an idiot would point a loaded gun at his foot and pull the trigger, and the manufacturer shouldn't be punished for the victim's stupidity.

But that defense would only have been good in a more responsible time. In a time when people were considered to be responsible for their own actions.

Today, that sort of thinking is no longer popular. It's much more comforting to consider yourself a victim of society, and to shift the blame from the guilty to the innocent.

That's partly the logic behind statutes that make parents responsible for their children's crimes. Yet Jewish law—Torah law—makes it clear that this should not be the case. We view criminal actions by the child as a rebellion against the parent, not as a result of defective child rearing. This is so to such a degree that the Torah demands death by stoning for a rebellious son. (Which, by the way, the Rabbis defined as a son who curses his parents, using the correct pronunciation of the divine name, in front of the appropriate witnesses, and so on, making it impossible to prove, and effectively removing the capital punishment.)

Jewish law considers a parent responsible for the child's wrongdoings only until the child reaches an age at which he or she can distinguish right from wrong. That is, until the age of *bar* or *bas mitzvah*. If, at 13, a child is considered capable of recognizing transgressions of Jewish religious law—which is enormously complicated—then he should certainly be capable of recognizing transgressions of civil law, which is much simpler.

In ancient Israel, of course, civil and religious law were the same thing. Theft was considered not only an offense against the victim, but was also an offense against God. The *Aseret Ha'Dibros*, after all, declares, *Lo tignov*, "do not steal." Refraining from stealing is declared a moral imperative, of equal stature with the prohibition of murder.[1]

1   It should be noted that the "stealing" referenced in the commandment is kidnapping, with the intent of selling the victim as a slave, and not the theft of ordinary property, which is treated elsewhere

Today, we extend childhood considerably. Until the 1950s, the appropriate age for a boy to enter the British Royal Navy, if he expected to become an officer, was 12. He'd enter the academy at that age, and in the early 19th century he would have gone to sea as a midshipman.

And, while it wasn't the custom in the United States to train military officers from so early an age, teenagers were expected to be responsible for their own actions.

When laws are proposed that make parents responsible for their children's criminal actions, we have a duty as Jews to oppose them—no matter how much they may appeal to our sense of justice. At least, we should oppose them when they deal with teenagers. Our tradition presumes that teenagers are old enough to tell right from wrong. More, it presumes that teenagers have free will, and make their own decisions.

The only way in which a parent could justly be held responsible for his child's action would be if the parent had ordered it. If a father tells his son to throw an egg at a neighbor's car, the father is responsible. If the son does it without such instruction, in what way can we blame the father?

Some writers have blamed psychiatry for many of the ills in the world today. No one, they say, ever feels guilty about anything. Or, if they do, they go into analysis and rationalize it.

An old stereotype was the Jewish mother complaining, "You never call." Today, the stereotype is more likely to be the son, who never *does* calls, rationalizing this by deciding that, when he calls, his mother always makes him feel guilty about not doing it often enough. His shrink has taught him that he should never feel guilty, so, obviously, it's really his mother's fault that he doesn't call. This makes him feel good. How it makes his mother feel is irrelevant because, in modern mental health, only your own feelings really matter.

It's like the way schools today base promotion on attendance, and ignore whether the students have actually learned anything. When I was in school, if you couldn't do the work, they kept you in the same grade for another year. Today, they think that holding a child back is bad for his self-esteem, so they promote him anyway.

Responsibility again. If the child does poorly in school, it's obviously the school's fault. Or the parents'.

There hasn't been an illegitimate child born in this country in the last 15 years. Now we just have children whose parents don't happen to be married. You can't stigmatize the child, who obviously had nothing to do with the problem. Yet, if we think back, it was only that stigma that kept the parents in line in the first place. We might say that the rest of the world has caught on to the Jewish tendency to deny the existence of a devil, but never picked up on our theme of personal responsibility. If you can't blame Satan, blame society itself.

But never—ever—blame the person who actually did it.

In the *L.A. Law* case, the jury tried to right what they perceived as a wrong by punishing an innocent relative of the actual guilty party. As Jews living in the United State, we are surrounded by a majority religion which is actually based on the belief that, no matter what you do, you can dump all the blame onto someone else, because you're never going to be morally strong enough to be responsible for yourself.

Yet the truth seems to be just the opposite. That we *are* responsible for our ourselves. That we cannot shift the blame if we do something wrong.

But until we all take that responsibility, and insist

that everyone else also takes responsibility for their own actions, things are just going to get worse.

D'var Torah: Acharei Mos/Kedoshim

[May 1, 1993] Our Torah portion for this week is once again taken from *Vayikra* [*Leviticus*], beginning with Chapter 16, verse 1, and ending with Chapter 20, verse 27. Like last week, we read two *sidros*.

Our first *sidrah* is *Acharei Mos*, a name meaning "after the death," and derived from the first sentence: *Vay'daber HaShem el Mosheh, acharei mos sh'nei b'nei Aharon...* "And God spoke to Moses after the death of Aaron's two sons..."

The second *sidrah*, *Kedoshim*, or "holy things," comes from God's command to the Israelite people, *K'doshim ti'yu, ki kadosh ani, HaShem Elokeichem*. "You shall be holy, for I am holy, the Lord your God."

Much of *Acharei Mos* is taken up with instructions for the ritual on Yom Kippur. But there are other laws contained here, and some are fascinating.

One of these has been a problem for every rabbi who has ever tried to give a complete explanation of the dietary laws. It states, "Any man of the children of Israel, or of the strangers living in your midst, who hunts beast or fowl which may be eaten, he shall pour out its blood and cover it with dust." [*Lev.* 17:13] The problem with this law is obvious. Classic rabbinic Judaism has long held that hunting is not permitted, and that animals killed by hunters are *treif*. Yet here the Torah seems clearly to say that hunting *is* allowed, and gives specific instructions on how the carcass is to be treated.

How can we reconcile these two points of view?

The truth is, most commentators simply ignore this passage. Other suggest that the verb usually translated as "hunt" actually means "trap," implying that the animal or bird is captured alive, so that the actual killing is done with the *shechitah* knife. Thus, the distinction between a wild and a domestic animal is only in whether the blood is simply poured out on the ground, or is also covered with dirt.

A few might also argue that no one today knows the exact procedure for pouring out and covering the blood of a hunted animal, so that this statute falls into the same category as eating locusts, in which a lack of knowledge as to which are actually the kosher species place all under a presumptive ban. If we don't know how to do it, we refrain lest we do it wrong.

It is here where we also find a passage that has been taken up by the Jehovah's Witnesses, to the potential harm of anyone who follows their interpretation. This is, "For the soul of all flesh is its blood, it is one with the soul; therefore I have said unto the children of Israel: the blood of any flesh you shall not eat; for the life of all flesh is its blood; anyone that eats it shall be cut off. [*Lev.* 17:14] This passage is the reason that the Witnesses refuse to allow blood transfusions.

For the physician, this presents an interesting dilemma. If a patient needs blood, and refuses it, the doctor violates a positive commandment: "You shall not stand idle while your neighbor bleeds." [*Lev.* 19:16]

Now, the Witnesses cite a number of passages, both

from Scripture, and from the primary work of Christian mythology, in an effort to support their mistaken belief. None of them do, because all refer to eating meat which has not been properly koshered, and have nothing to do with taking blood into a vein.

Ethically, it presents a Jewish doctor with a major problem. If the doctor doesn't give the blood, and the patient dies because of this, the doctor could be considered guilty of murder by omission. On the other hand, one could also argue that the patient has committed suicide, which is equally wrong.

Except for some very rare circumstances, we consider suicide to be inherently irrational. Jewish law forbids holding a funeral for a suicide. The fact that nearly all who kill themselves actually receive a normal funeral is based on the rabbinic dictum that suicide is, in itself, considered proof that the victim was insane. Since the insane cannot be held responsible for their actions, a funeral is permitted. *Halakhich* suicide is defined very narrowly, so that the precise circumstances rarely occur.

Ethically, a Jewish doctor would be required to give the blood, regardless of the patient's wishes, on the grounds that we are forbidden to help a person take his own life. Particularly when the suicidal behavior is based on a misinterpretation of a law which applies only to Jews, and has no relevance at all for any sort of Christian.

Such decisions are, however, more likely to be based on the advice of malpractice attorneys, who tend to favor letting the patient be the boss, even when he isn't really competent to make the decision. Civil law will probably also be on the patient's side, under statutes that allow adults to act stupidly as long as they can cite a religious reason to do so.

One of the more interesting passages in *Kedoshim*,

our second *sidrah*, forbids a court to favor a poor man over a rich man. [Lev. 19:15] This sounds odd today, when we tend to think that the courts are weighted in favor of the rich.

The opposite, of course, is really true. This is particularly so in civil cases, where juries too often find against a wealthy defendant simply because they think that he can afford to pay, and the other guy doesn't have anything. Rather like the case in which an automobile company was forced to pay a judgment many times greater than the actual earning potential of a man killed in one of its cars. The jury, in effect, stuck it to the car company and rewarded the victim's family for the good luck of having their son die in one of that company's cars.

The Torah position is that justice must be even handed. The wealth, or poverty, of the litigants is not to be considered. We are commanded to be scrupulously fair, and not try to right perceived inequities.

Our *sidrah* also demands equal justice for both citizen and foreigner. For Jew and non-Jew. We are reminded that we were ill treated when we were foreigners in Egypt, and that true justice demands that we learn from what has happened to us, and not become oppressors ourselves.

We also find definitions of various sorts of incest, which might make a good adult education subject sometime.

The central core of these *sidros* is justice. This is very pronounced in traditional Jewish law. Justice for all: Jew or gentile, rich or poor, strong or weak. And while justice is the ideal, it is up to us to see that it is upheld for all.

Cults

[May 7, 1993] Cults have been in the news recently. There was the siege in Waco, with its fiery end. Articles have appeared in the papers, trying to define cults. In the past week there was a TV movie about a particularly vicious cult leader, and an *Unsolved Mysteries* segment about a cult leader who vanished trying to avoid prosecution for rape, seemingly taking the entire cult with him.

The hardest question to answer about cults is also the most basic. Just what *is* a cult? After Jonestown, Congress held some hearings in an effort to define cults, and to separate them from legitimate religions. But they failed to arrive at a definition. No matter what characteristic they came up with, it could also usually be applied to aspects of legitimate religion.

Cults, for instance, believe that their particular concept of God is the only correct one, and that all others are, in some way, wrong. But so does every other religion. Jews believe that God is absolutely One, and cannot be divided. Moslems claim to believe this, but also include a belief in a powerful devil as the source for all that is evil, so, in effect, they add a second god. The very declaration of omnipotence requires that any enemy be equally omnipotent. So, if he is able to fight a war against God, Satan also has to *be* a god.

Christians split the divine into three parts, with most of the emphasis on the three rather than the one. Hindus believe that there is only one god, but run him through many incarnations, and create a pantheon consisting of hundreds of separate incarnations of the same divine being.

The one common factor is that each faith believes it is correct, and the others are wrong. If we didn't think they were wrong, after all, why would we be so stubborn in maintaining our separate existence?

Another characteristic of a cult is that the leader is seen as possessing some special knowledge. The members tend to do whatever their leader asks, without raising any real questions. But, again, such obedience can also be found in some more legitimate settings. The Lubavitcher Rebbe was known for telling his followers that they should pick up and move to various places. Most of the time they did. The congregation in Fort Myers was established in exactly that way, about two years ago. The Rebbe sent a young rabbi and several families in what amounted to setting up a Chabad mission to the non-chassidic community that existed there.

One thing that Christian cults do seem to have in common is an obsession with sex. Very often, sex is seen as something to be shunned by everyone except the leader.

David Koresh seems to have considered it perfectly okay for himself to have dozens of wives. He was known to split up couples, taking the women for himself. Since his followers considered him inherently divine, most of them accepted this.

Ervil LeBaron, who was profiled in a TV movie this week, took an even more extreme outlook. He called himself a prophet, and made it very clear that whatever he said, or whatever he wanted done, was the will of God. If he wanted to add a particular woman to his harem, and she preferred someone else, he would simply have his rival killed. He justified his actions by reference to a higher law.

This may be one of the points where cults and religions split. Normal rabbis, ministers, and priests can tell people to do something, but if the person doesn't want to, we lack any real enforcement power. I might prefer that the entire congregation keep kosher homes, drive only to the synagogue and back home again on *shabbos*, and refrain from writing, using the telephone, or watching television on *shabbos*. I might prefer it, but the only person in this sanctuary that I can actually order to do these things with any expectation of obedience is me.

In cults, obedience is a given. The leader has absolute power, and anyone who disobeys will be subjected to harsh discipline. Expulsion from the cult is often thought of as an ultimate punishment. Cult members believe that their group is the only one that will be admitted to heaven. Anyone outside the group is doomed to eternal punishment. To be expelled from the group is, really, to be sentenced to hell.

And some cults go even farther. LeBaron killed everyone who disagreed with him. There is a feeling that, even though LeBaron is now dead, some of his followers are still killing off his enemies.

David Koresh, like many Christian cult leaders, was obsessed with the book of *Revelation*. Even though the characters named in *Revelation* have been dead for centuries, and the entire eschatological premise of the book thoroughly disproven, it still exerts a strong influence even on normative Christianity.

In the hands of cult leaders, it is particularly dangerous. Since *Revelation* speaks of terrible things happening in the end times, the cult leaders feel justified in *doing* some fairly awful things. Koresh had built up quite an arsenal, and was rumored to be converting semi-automatic weapons—which are perfectly legal—into fully-automatic weapons, which are not.

One group has constructed a huge bomb shelter, expecting nuclear war at any moment. A constant fear is that when the end of the world prophecies espoused by these groups fail, they will try to find a way to make them happen. The only difficult thing about building an atomic bomb, after all, is getting your hands on the fissionable material for the core. Kids have built nuclear weapons as high school science projects that would have worked if they had the proper materials.

This may be one of the greatest dangers in cults. They absolutely believe that they are right, and that everyone else is not only wrong, but a tool of Satan. Whatever actions they take, no matter how wrong, can be justified by the leader's special status. Since God speaks through the leader, the leader has to be right. Anyone who disagrees with the leader is not only wrong, but evil. Possibly even deserving of death.

There is always a danger whenever a group becomes too authoritarian, or too dogmatic. Absolutism in belief often translates into self-justification of the unacceptable. The murder of a Florida doctor by an abortion protester is simply one example. The justification of the murder by a number of people supposedly representing legitimate religious views is another. These are, supposedly, mainstream religious types. If they can justify murder, how much easier would it be for someone in a fringe cult, whose very concepts of right and wrong are formulated by their leader to serve his or her own purposes?

I don't think there are any easy solutions here. We find it hard to even define cults. Education isn't always the answer, because the cult's appeal is more likely to be psychological than rational, and facts don't always affect emotions.

About all we can do, really, is try to remain alert, spot dangerous trends, and warn people when we see them.

Do You Believe in God?

[May 15, 1993] The pilot for the old Sherman Hemsley TV show *Amen* began with a fictional Philadelphia church searching for a new minister. The board was obviously interested in the candidate's qualifications for the job, so they asked him all the usual questions. Religious philosophy, where he went to school, previous pulpits. All the things you'd expect to ask someone who wanted to become your spiritual leader.

Hemsley's character, Deacon Frye, puts the final question to the minister. He asks him, "Do you believe in God?"

It got a big laugh. It was supposed to. After all, what sort of kook asks a clergyman if he believes in God?

Yet, if someone were to ask the same question of each of us, how would we answer?

For more than 3,000 years, we have believed that the Torah contains both the word and law of God. We sometimes suggest that parts are of human authorship. There is one theory of Torah origination that suggests that only the legal content was literally dictated on Sinai, leaving Moses to fill in the historical narrative from oral traditions.

The oldest tradition declares that the entire Torah, from the first word of *Bereshis* to the final word of

Devarim, was dictated by God while Moses was on Sinai. A *midrash* on this tradition states that, as he wrote the final words, Moses wept. An understandable reaction, as he would then be writing about his own death.

But there's a problem with this tradition. The idea that the entire Torah was given at one time, only a few weeks after the exodus, presents us with a God-concept at odds with our usual beliefs. If the entire Torah was given on Sinai, everything that happened from then until the entry into *Eretz Yisroel* was pre-ordained. It was all going to happen in exactly that way, and there was nothing that could change this.

This is the opposite of free will. If we believe in free will, then we also have to believe that the choices are our own. We have to believe that each individual, in every situation, has the power to make a conscious choice between good and evil.

And this is a distinctly Jewish idea. We have the power to choose between the *yetzer tov* and the *yetzer ha'ra*—the good and the evil impulse. Both are always present, and it is up to us which we will listen to. This is the very meaning of free will.

Many people have a hard time reconciling an omniscient and omnipotent God with the idea of free will. They want to know how God can be all-powerful and all-knowing if people get to make their own choices. The most logical answer to this seems to be that God knows what the result of every possible action will be, but does *not* know—willfully doesn't allow himself to know—which of these myriad actions we will take. It's rather like the old science fiction concept of alternate universes. Each time we do something we create an alternate universe, one in which we did this thing, and another in which we didn't.

The idea of free will, however, applies only if the

Torah was given in the manner the text describes. From time to time Moses would enter the *Mishkan* and put various questions to God. So, over the course of 40 years, the entire text was revealed, and the history compiled. If not—if the whole text was dictated at one time on Sinai—we are presented with a diminished God. A God who first causes people to break a law, and then punishes them for doing so. It's like the idea of a cop holding a gun to someone's head, forcing him to hold up a liquor store, and then arresting him for doing it.

Our tradition says that we will be forgiven if we repent, but repentance can only exist with free will. If we are just following a script, our actions are not our own, and it would be pointless to feel sorry about anything we've ever done.

There seems to be a great tendency for people to suddenly get religion while they're in jail. Mostly these are born-again Christians. But we also find Jews following the same pattern, and suddenly turning Orthodox in jail.[2]

There's nothing wrong with this. Some people really do change. The first time he was governor of Ohio, James Rhodes staffed his official residence with a high percentage of convicted murderers. Someone had done a study, and discovered that people who commit second degree murder are the least likely to ever commit another crime.[3]

---

2   This was written in the early 1990s. Today, the newly religious incarcerated also include a high percentage of Moslems. An obvious difference is that most of these prison-religious Moslems were not Islamic when they entered prison, but were converted after they were there.

3   This probably has less to do with the crime than with the criminal. Second degree murder—the unplanned but deliberate killing of another person—is most often a "crime of passion," and most likely to be committed by someone who normally wouldn't step outside the bounds of the law. In other words, it's a

So how do we know if a person has really changed? Most of the time, we don't. But if he says that he has, we are actually required by Jewish law to believe him. This derives from the Talmudic principle that one who imposes a prejudice against himself is to be believed. That is, if a man tells you that he was a criminal, but has now reformed, he should be believed because he didn't *have* to admit to being an ex-criminal in the first place.

The same principle applies to a woman who has lost her *get*, and wishes to remarry. Since she could have lied and said that she had never been married, she is to be believed when she says that she has a *get*, but has lost it.

But these principles, again, really work only if we believe in a higher power. Belief in God is one of the factors that make us live a moral life. What, after all, keeps us on the path of righteousness? Are we afraid our neighbors won't approve of our actions? Think about it. Our neighbors often disapprove of what we do, but it hardly ever keeps us from doing it.

If we can read the Torah, and then say to ourselves, "This really doesn't apply to me," then whatever we do is going to be moral in our own eyes. Even if it clearly isn't moral by Torah law.

The official who was in charge of torture in medieval Nürnberg once said that, "Morality is an expression of expediency." In other words, human moral standards are based on convenience. If a moral standard becomes inconvenient, it will be discarded.

It is for exactly this reason that we, as Jews, derive our moral standards from the Torah. We don't rely on

---

crime usually committed by a non-criminal, who is as likely to be as horrified at the outcome as anyone else once he calms down. The police don't usually have to look very hard to catch these people, because as often as not they don't try to run and expect to be punished.

human judgment for what is moral. We look to a higher authority.

If someone asks if we believe in God, we could say that they are really asking if we believe in a permanent, unchanging moral standard. They are asking if we believe that there is always someone watching us, so that our private actions take on the same importance as our public actions.

Our behavior is clearly influenced by our beliefs. If we really believe in God, then we will mold our actions accordingly.

In Judaism, we usually consider actions more important than belief. Yet the very root of those actions is found in belief. It is possible to be a good person, and even to be quite observant, without believing. But it is much easier if you also believe.

A *mitzvah* is not, after all, a good deed. It is something that you do because it is demanded of you. When we say that it's a *mitzvah* to attend a funeral, we don't mean that this would be a nice thing if you don't have anything better to do. We mean that Jewish law demands that you attend, because it is a *mitzvah*—a commandment—to honor the dead.

Even if we don't always think of it in that way, belief is the essence of Judaism. If we don't believe, then all we are doing is going through a meaningless ritual. If we do believe, then everything we do has meaning within the bounds of our ancient covenant. And this is what we should aim for. A life *with* meaning.

End of Days

[May 21, 1993] Flipping through the channels the other day, I was confronted with yet another showing of a pseudo-religious documentary on one of the so-called "religious" channels. This was a film version of Hal Lindsay's book, *The Late, Great Planet Earth.*

The film's credibility suffered right from the first scene, which was supposed to depict the stoning of a "false prophet" in ancient Israel. It was all typically Hollywood. A crowd of angry people chase the victim up a mountain until he can't run any farther. Then they throw a few hundred rocks at him.

It's dramatic, but it's about as realistic as a western in which the pioneers circle their Chevy station wagons and fight off the Indians with M-16s.

A real stoning was a judicial execution, carried out only after a proper trial, and conducted according to strict rules. Like all forms of capital punishment under Jewish law, a stoning was intended to be as close to painless as possible. The first stone had to be of at least a certain weight, was always thrown at the back of the head, from no farther than about three feet, and the intent was to either kill the victim instantly, or at least render him unconscious during the rest of the procedure.

The inaccurate treatment of the stoning in the film

is symptomatic of its whole theme. Distortion is presented as fact. And only that "evidence" that seems to support a predetermined outcome is presented.

Hal Lindsay, who wrote the book, and who appears in the film, is what is termed an "end time" theologian. In other words, he believes that the apocalyptic prophecies found in the Bible are about to be fulfilled, and the world — as we know it — will shortly end.

And, like most theologians who stress these "end of the world" ideas, he has absolutely no interest in *averting* the end. His whole emphasis is on *preparing for* the end. Which, in his writing, involves adopting Lindsay's interpretation of Christian theology.

Now, the whole idea of Apocalypse isn't new. There was a whole school of Jewish apocalyptic literature. The best known examples are found in *Daniel*. Christians add *Revelation*, an alternate title for which has always been *Apocalypse*.

Many other apocalyptic books never made it into the canon of either faith. The Sages excluded anything written after about 400 BCE from the Jewish canon. The early Church Fathers seem to have picked *Revelation* for inclusion precisely because it was so obscurely written than when the predicted events failed to happen, it could be re-interpreted into a different time period.

The premise of all apocalyptic literature, canonical or not, is that the world as we know it is about to end. The author gives a reason for the coming destruction — virtually always because humanity is corrupt and wallowing in sin. He also give the signs that will indicate the end is near. These are generally a series of natural disasters, coupled with a war of some sort. He then concludes with a description of the world that will replace this one.

There is also, of course, an indication of just who can

be expected to survive. The apocalypse never destroys the planet, after all, just the people who don't meet the author's standard of righteousness.

Hal Lindsay's books, which collect these prophecies and attempt to relate them to current events, are actually just a part of a modern revival of the apocalyptic school. The book David Koresh was supposedly working on was another example.

One of the more interesting examples came out a few years ago. I may even still have a copy, since it was very widely circulated by people who really should have known better. The author of this work *proved*, with absolute certainty, that the world was going to end of Rosh Ha'Shanah, 5749 [September 12/13, 1988].

Which it obviously didn't. He followed that up with a new edition, in which he discovered he'd made a math error, and the world would really end on Rosh Ha'Shanah 5750 *[September 30/October 1, 1989]*. If he's discovered any further errors in the last three years, he seems to have kept quiet about them.

All of these modern doom-sayers have the same problem with getting their version of the end to come true. They all begin with the book of *Revelation*, and, because they do, their theories instantly founder in a sea of irrelevance. Since *Revelation* is based on nothing but mythology, prophecies based on that book are no more likely to be accurate than prophecies based on something Apollo supposedly said to Heracles.

The Hebrew prophets never really went in for long-range predictions. Isaiah spoke mainly of events which would take place in his own lifetime. The "Emmanuel" prophecy [*Isaiah* 7:14-16], for instance, is linked directly to the siege of Jerusalem during the reign of Achaz, and becomes utterly meaningless if you try to apply it outside that brief period. The 53rd chapter of

Isaiah, which Christian theologians have interpreted as prefiguring the life of their messianic candidate, is actually written in the past tense. And, as Ibn Ezra pointed out, it could just as easily describe the life of Jeremiah.

Even Isaiah's seemingly long range prediction that Israel would be freed from captivity by Cyrus of Persia is long-range only if we presume that it was written by the *first* Isaiah, who lived a century before the Babylonian exile. On the other hand, if it was written by the *second* Isaiah, who was a contemporary of Cyrus, the "prediction" is little more than a report of current—or very nearly current—events.

When asked to explain why they think the End Time is now, modern apocalyptic theorists cite recent increases in the number of earthquakes, floods, famines, wars, and plagues, along with a terrible increase in crime. All of these things were predicted as harbingers of the end.

But it's another false premise. There are no more natural disasters happening now than there have been in any other historic period. And, as dangerous as we may think they are, the streets today are far safer than they were at the turn of the century. Almost two millennia ago, the Sages made certain additions to the services so that the congregation could return home from the synagogue on *shabbos* eve as a group. It was considered too dangerous to walk home alone.

There have always been earthquakes. But in ancient times, only local quakes were noticed. Today, even an earthquake like the one in Ohio a few years ago, which was less noticeable than a passing train, makes the national news. We don't have more disasters, we just have better reporting.

Famine has been a constant companion to humanity throughout history, with changing weather patterns affecting crops. Floods also follow these long-term weather patterns, because people build on flood plains during prolonged dry periods, then are flooded out when the next wet cycle begins. It's a bit like the way Italians keep rebuilding on the slopes of Vesuvius. They know the volcano will eventually erupt again, but they figure it won't happen in *their* lifetime.

The single common fault that runs through nearly all apocalyptic literature is that it presumes that God blew it when he gave humanity free will. This carries with it the equally false presumption that God is eventually going to have to "correct" his "mistake" and establish direct rule. Apocalyptic theories are mostly produced by people with a very pessimistic view of the world in general and humanity in particular.

The core of "end time" scenarios is the questioning of humanity's ability to solve its own problems without divine intervention of a grand scale. On the other hand, the true root of messianic hope is just the opposite. It's a belief that humanity *will* solve its own problems, thereby creating a perfected world and a messianic age. Rather than wait for God to ask, it's up to us to bring peace to the world.

Rather than give in to the pessimism of the doom sayers, we have to get to work on ourselves. For a perfected world is, really, nothing more than a world in which every individual has learned to live in harmony with everyone else. The whole is the sum of the parts.

And the parts, the individuals who will make up this collective whole, are us.

A Sense of Compulsion

[May 28, 1993] One of the most misused words in the Jewish vocabulary is *mitzvah*. How do we commonly use that word? Most of the time, it takes on the meaning of "good deed."

Yet, if we look in the Torah, how many of the 613 *mitzvos* really seem to be good deeds? Is refraining from murder nothing more than a courtesy? Conversely, would we consider it a good deed to execute someone for gathering firewood on *shabbos*? Is it a good deed to kill every man, woman, child, and animal in a conquered Canaanite city?

Yet all are *mitzvos*.

A number of rabbis have, in recent years, complained that something is missing in the Jews of today. Too many of us seem to be lacking a sense of compulsion. A sense that we should do certain things, not because they seem right, but because we have been given a divine mandate to do them.

One of the classic examples of the "right" reason for doing something is a story told of Rabbi Akiva. Traditional Jews tend to develop what is sometimes called a "Jewish stomach." The very idea of eating pork, or meat cooked with milk or butter, makes them physically ill.

One of Rabbi Akiva's disciples remarked on this.

That it would make him sick to eat pork, which was utterly disgusting. But Rabbi Akiva told him that he had it all wrong. "Do not say, 'I do not eat pork because I find it repulsive.' Rather, say that, 'While its taste be sweet to me, I do not eat it because the Holy One, blessed be he, has commanded me not to'."

In the generation that came to this country from eastern Europe, it wasn't uncommon to find men who would change jobs every week. Their sense of what was demanded of them by God would not permit them to work on *shabbos*, even if refusing to do so meant they would be fired. A great impetus toward the entrepreneurial spirit among the Jewish men of that generation was the realization that, if you owned the business, you could close it on *shabbos*.

Contrast that with today. How many people today absolutely refuse to work on *shabbos?* The Torah, after all, makes it clear that those who do should be put to death. It even tells of the execution of a sabbath violator during the period after the exodus.

Now, so far as anyone knows, that single incident seems to have been the only time this happened. The Sages taught that the death penalty for violating the sabbath would thereafter be in the form of *kares*, which is interpreted to mean "death from heaven." For each *shabbos* a person worked, he might lose one day of his total allotment. If you worked every *shabbos* for ten years, your life span might be shortened by 520 days. Or, perhaps, it would be 520 hours. Or 520 minutes. The Rabbis and Sages were unclear as to exactly what was involved, but they were clear that any violation of certain *mitzvos* brought an early death.

It has been suggested that what is needed in Judaism today is a restoration of that sense of compulsion. That we need to look at the *mitzvos* as "commandments," which is what they are, and not as "good deeds," which they clearly are not. Nor should we be frightened by the number of *mitzvos*. The Sages determined that there were 613 *mitzvos*. But most of these do not apply to the majority of Jews. Many operate only in the land of Israel, as they concern agriculture in that land. Some apply only to *kohanim*, and then only while they are serving in the Temple. Some apply only to a king. Some apply only to men, or only to women. Some apply only to someone who is married. A few apply only to those who are in the process of divorcing.

Less than 100 apply to everyone.

Most of those that apply aren't that hard to do. We are taught, for instance, that we should say at least 150 *b'rachos* each day. It sounds like a lot, but you actually say most of them during the three daily services. The rest come with fairly ordinary acts, such as eating and drinking, or washing our hands, or even going to the bathroom. Yes, there's even a blessing for that—it's in our *siddur*[4] at the top of page 44, and is a part of the series of blessings we are supposed to say upon arising in the morning.

Some *mitzvos* might even seem a little dangerous. The Torah demands, "Do not stand idle while your neighbor bleeds." At its most literal, we could interpret this to mean that, if we see someone being attacked, we must come to their aid. Less directly, we might interpret this to mean that it is our duty to help whenever life is in peril. Whether this means trying to stop a mugging, or protesting ethnic cleansing in Bosnia, or giving blood

---

[4] *Sabbath and Festival Prayer Book*, 1946, 1973, The Rabbinical Assembly of America and The United Synagogue of America. This has since been replaced in many Conservative congregations by the *Siddur Sim Shalom*, which is slightly larger, has somewhat clearer typography, and takes more of a feminist outlook in the liturgy.

when it is needed. (Which it usually is.) In the last case, not standing idle while our neighbor bleeds means, literally, providing the blood to replace what is lost.

In all these instances, our actions, or even our words, may save lives. God, after all, cares for all of humanity. When the Egyptians drowned in the sea after Israel had crossed over in safety, and the Israelites were rejoicing, the angels wished to join in the celebration. Yet God rebuked them, saying, "How can you sing, when my creatures are drowning?"

And if God cares even for those who would harm his Chosen People, how much more must he care for the majority of people who lack that special malice? And are we not, also, commanded to love our neighbor as ourselves?

Does not the Torah demand that, if an enemy's animal falls into a pit, or collapses under its burden, we must set aside our dislike of the owner and help the animal? Even join with our enemy to save it?

And isn't this somewhat contrary to human nature? It seems only natural to want our enemy to fail. To see him heaped with misfortune. To see his business deals collapse, and his wife run off with someone else.

It seems natural. But it's wrong. In a *midrash*, the story was told of a man who would sin, and then repent and ask to be forgiven. Yet, as soon as he was forgiven, he would go out and sin again. And, each time, he would repent his actions, and be forgiven again, and then sin again, and so on. And the angels asked God, "How many times must this man be forgiven?" The reply was, "One more time than he asks."

It isn't easy to keep forgiving your enemies. But, if they ask, you are required to do so. It isn't easy to do a lot of the things that the Torah demands of us as Jews. It isn't easy to regain that sense of compulsion. That sense of the mandatory. But, if we are to be the people God expects us to be, we need to regain it.

Reacting to Others

[June 4, 1993] Have you ever watched a good actor at work? If you have, then you may have noticed that the key to a good performance isn't so much what the actor does, as how he reacts to the other actors. Not action, but reaction.

The space shuttle goes up into space because the engines exert a *downward* force. And since the downward force of the engines is greater than the weight of the shuttle, the shuttle reacts by rising.

We tend to think of reaction as operating mainly in the area of physics, or of human relations. We don't often think of religions as reacting. Yet each faith in influenced by its surroundings.

In his book, *Death and Birth of Judaism*[5], Jacob Neusner developed the theme that what we perceive as traditional Judaism is actually a reaction to the Christian dominance of the Roman Empire in the early 4th century. Professor Neusner looks into the Talmud and concludes that the earliest part, the *Mishnah*, was compiled by men who were unconcerned with the opinions of the non-Jewish world. But he believes that the *Gemarah*, the elaborate commentary on the *Mishnah* which completes

---
5   Neusner, Jacob. *Death and Birth of Judaism.* New York: Basic Books, 1987.

the Talmud, shows the reactions of men whose basic beliefs were being called into question.

From the time of Abraham until the reign of Constantine, Judaism never really had to justify itself. Jews dominated the land of Israel. We had our own kings. We lived in accordance with our own laws. The opinions of the gentiles were of little concern to the Sages, because the gentiles were a dwindling minority.

But when Constantine made the Roman Empire officially Christian in 345, things changed. Christian theologians argued that their very political dominance was proof of the validity of their beliefs. They claimed that Jews and Judaism were anachronistic, and should now disappear.

The Rabbis developed a religious philosophy that rejected Christian teaching without ever actually referring to it. Rather than argue that a specific individual was not the messiah, we argued that the condition of the world proved that the messiah was yet to come. Our interpretations made it clear that Judaism remained a living faith which had never been supplanted.

Traditional Judaism is based on the concept of the two Torahs. The Torah *sh'bik'tav*, or "written Torah"—the actual scroll we read from on *shabbos* morning; and the Torah *sh'ba'al peh*, or "oral Torah." Our Rabbis and Sages taught that this "oral Torah" was also given to Moses on Sinai, and passed on by word of mouth until the time of Yehuda *ha'nasi*, who committed the *Mishnah* to writing during a period of persecution, lest it be lost through the deaths of its masters.

Yet the concept of the dual Torah isn't found in the *Mishnah*. It is first developed in the *Gemarah*, many years later.

And the *Gemarah*, as I said earlier, is often reactive to the surrounding culture, while the *Mishnah* assumes a

Jewish cultural base.

Let me cite a more recent example of a tradition which, on closer examination, is actually a reaction to gentile dominance. In the early 19th century the Orthodox rabbinate in Berlin complained to the civil authorities that the early Reform rabbis were violating Jewish tradition by preaching weekly vernacular sermons. Preaching sermons, the Orthodox rabbis firmly declared, was contrary to Jewish tradition, which limited a rabbi to two sermons a year, and on very specific subjects.

The Reform rabbis—and, let's remember, what in Germany and England is called Reform, we call Conservative—countered this attack by an appeal to history. They found that preaching sermons was a common practice in Talmudic times. The great Sages and Rabbis were all excellent preachers. That was how they gathered their followings. But when Christianity became the state religion of Rome, Jewish preaching was forbidden. The Church had put pressure on the government to stop it, because rabbinic preaching helped to keep the Jews knowledgeable about their faith, and the Church wanted them ignorant and easier to convert.

After all, it's much easier to convince someone he holds a wrong opinion about something if he doesn't know why he believes that way in the first place. It's like the way my Colombian ex-mother-in-law lights candles every Friday night, soaks and salts her meat before cooking it, and never allows leavened bread on the table on Easter, yet has absolutely no idea of just why she does these things, and would be rather appalled by anyone pointing out that she was simply following the customs of long-forgotten Jewish ancestors.

Tradition, in other words, has to be supported by knowledge, or it loses its meaning. Or, as in the case of

Jewish preaching, takes on a totally different aspect as a reaction to an outside force. The tradition said that sermons were not allowed, not out of any Jewish dislike for the practice, but because our persecutors forbade them. Over time, the reason was forgotten, and all that remained was the incorrect notion that rabbis didn't give sermons.

The conception of Judaism as a religion also seems to be a reaction to Christian political dominance. The majority faith put pressure on us to convert, and we reacted by erecting a fence around the commandments. By hedging in our lives with a complex set of law that insured our survival, even as they served to isolate us from a hostile environment. As long as we held tightly to these laws and beliefs, our identity as Jews remained secure.

Today, Judaism is changing again. In many ways we are returning to an older definition of Jewishness. A pre-Talmudic definition, where Jewish identity is more ethnic or nationalistic, and not so much religious. Israel once again exists on her historic soil. And, in Israel at least, a Jew isn't required to define himself by comparison to gentiles. He is surrounded by other Jews. He lives in a Jewish world.

In the United States, the majority of people are obviously not Jewish. Equally, the Church exerts no direct political power. If there is persecution, we can actually demand that the government do something about it. The government has a mandate to *stop* persecution. Far different from the "old country," where the government was just as often the instigator.

Because we live in a free country, our perceptions are different from those of Jews living in many other parts of the world. Young Jews, who grew up in the '60s and after, have different perceptions from their parents.

Where the older generation might ask, "What would the gentiles think?" the younger generation is more apt to say, "Who *cares* what they think, as long as we're right?"

Where once the reaction to a relatively benign prejudice, such as housing restrictions, or hotel accommodations, was to just go along with the system, the reaction today is a loud assertion of the injustice involved, and a quick action toward correcting it.

Today, when there is a general religious revival in this country, Judaism is also experiencing a revival. We are taking our faith a little more seriously. We're looking to find ways of reinforcing our Jewish identity. It may be nothing more than lighting *shabbos* candles, or being a little more careful with our diets, or even giving Jewish names to our children, but more and more of us are doing it.

It's another form of reaction. And because it makes us more conscious of ourselves as Jews, it's also the sort of reaction we need.

Programming

[August 6, 1993] Technology can be a wonderful thing. You can do things with modern computers, for instance, that are practically impossible without them. Calculations that would take decades to accomplish on paper can be performed in a few minutes on a powerful computer.

Yet, sometimes, there are shortcomings. Some time ago, I worked with a friend on a piece of music. We programmed it into his computer. It took several hours, until all of the harmonies were exactly right, and the finished piece sounded the way we wanted it to.

And this was when we made a discovery. This wonderful music composition program lacked a single feature. You could play the music on the computer's tone generator—or you could play it on an electronic keyboard with the use of a special interface. But you could *not* make a printed copy!

So, after all that work, we still had to sit in front of the screen and copy the music onto manuscript paper with a pencil.

You can't fault the computer. It did exactly what the program told it to do. Nor can you really fault the program. No doubt the person who wrote it also sells a *separate* graphics program, which could be used to print it. An axiom in computing is that, the less a program costs, the more likely you are to need to buy additional programs to get the full use out of it.

As complex as they seem, computers are very simple devices. A computer can tell the difference between a "one" and a "zero." That's all. By stringing ones and zeros together, in a particular order, the computer creates readable information.

But the one thing we have to remember is that computers are incapable of thinking. They do only what they're told to do. Someone writes a program, loads it into the computer, and the computer follows the instructions.

And it often seems as if people work in the same way. We like to think that we guide our own destiny, making all of our decisions based upon our own, innate wisdom and knowledge. In fact, we are often just reacting to early programming. No one develops racial, ethnic, or religious prejudices based on rational, objective observation. If we dislike a particular group of people, it's usually because we were taught to do so as children.

In the musical *South Pacific*, Oscar Hammerstein had one of the characters attempt to explain the roots of prejudice in the song, *You've Got to be Carefully Taught*.[6] It's this sort of teaching that creates the early programming of our own minds. Our own internal computer software.

It has often been said that, if you teach a child while he or she is still young, they will not stray far from that teaching. And this is generally true.

---

6 When originally delivered, this sermon included quoted lyrics from the song. These are not included here due to potential copyright issues.

The problem is that it is just as easy to teach the wrong things as the right ones. Maybe even easier.

A lot of people believe in conspiracies. They think there are vast, secret organizations that really run the world, and manipulate events down to the smallest detail. In their world coincidences don't exist.

In John D. McDonald's novel *Condominium*, there was a noisy but minor character who firmly believed that there was an enormous Jewish conspiracy to take over the world. He had spent many years collecting "evidence." Mostly, this was in the form of newspaper and magazine clippings, which were connected only by the workings of his particular psychosis. And when a tremendous hurricane roared in to destroy his building, he died convinced that this was the final proof of his ideas, because it was obvious—to him—that the Rothschilds had found a way to create a hurricane and aim it directly at him to destroy his evidence.

This character was actually a fairly typical example of a conspiracy believer. He was an essentially weak individual. He was afraid of nearly everything. Much too aware that the actions of any particular individual generally have very little effect on history. (Or, at least, little obvious effect.) And he was conscious, too, of the seemingly random chance that rules a world he believed had to be a much more ordered place.

People like this believe in conspiracies because they offer an explanation. If your stock values drop, it's never because you bought the wrong stock. It's because a secret block of financiers are manipulating the stock prices at your expense. If the price of corn goes up, it's still the result of a conspiracy. The lousy crop was caused by global conspirators who have a secret means of manipulating the weather.

It's simply easier to handle the problems of life when

you can blame them on someone else. And, if you have to find someone to blame, you make it someone who is different from yourself. Preferably someone weaker.

You blame a minority.

When a young woman jogging in Central Park was attacked by a group of teenagers a few years ago, it was the *victim* who was blamed by many. It was argued that she had provoked the attack by being there. The attackers *were* charged. If I remember correctly, they were even convicted. But far too many people still faulted the victim for being in a "dangerous" place at the wrong time of day.

Most conspiracy theories follow a similar line of reasoning. The blame should be attached to the victim.

I don't believe in blaming victims. It wasn't that young woman's fault that she was raped and nearly beaten to death. She had a perfect right to be where she was. It was the gang that attacked her who were at fault. Totally.

The truth is, a victim *never* contributes to a crime simply by happening to be in the same place as a criminal. Only the criminal makes a choice to commit a crime.

Early teaching. Prejudice. All of these affect us to some degree. But we also have free will. We have to make our own decisions. Any group, no matter how large, is made up of a collection of individuals. And each individual has to make his or her own choices. Do you go along with the group? Or do you follow your own course?

Regardless of the opinions of so-called experts, no one ever becomes a criminal through environment, or poverty, or other external causes. Someone becomes a criminal because he has made a personal choice to *be* a criminal. Because he's decided that it's easier to steal than to work.

It all comes down to making choices. When we are faced with a choice between right and wrong, it's up to us to choose what is right.

It's also up to us to teach our children, and to teach those around us, to recognize the difference, and to make the right choices.

Abortion and Suicide

[August 20, 1993] I'm finding interesting things in the news lately. Doctor Kevorkian has been arrested for helping a young man kill himself.[7] A so-call right to lifer tried to kill another doctor yesterday. And a Catholic priest in Alabama has been reprimanded by his bishop for suggesting that it would be okay if good Christians went around killing any doctors who were performing abortions.

There is a mutual exclusivity in the idea of shooting obstetricians, which nearly all doctors performing abortions are. The idea is that, if you kill the doctor, you save the lives of his victims. On the other hand, if you kill him, you also condemn yourself. In effect, you're saying, "I'm going to murder this person, so that he won't murder this other person."

And yet, is it actually murder? Catholic dogma insists that a separate person, endowed with all rights, exists from the moment of conception. Yet, in the Torah, God treats the killing of a pregnant woman as murder, subject to the death penalty, but considers the killing of an

---

7   Doctor Jack Kevorkian (1928–2011), was arrested several times for assisting at a suicide, but was generally either not charged or acquitted until 1998, when he was convicted of second degree murder.

unborn child as a civil matter, to be settled by the payment of a fine to the woman's husband.

Our law considers a child to be a separate person only after the head has been delivered. Until that time, the life of the mother always takes precedence.

The Catholic Church never looked at it that way. Their ban on abortion has always been total. Even years ago, when abortion was illegal in this country except to save the mother's life, the Church forbade it. The policy in Catholic hospitals was that, if the mother would die unless the pregnancy was terminated, the mother was to be allowed to die rather than abort the fetus. Their doctrine didn't permit the doctor to choose one over the other. The whole issue was to be left in the hands of God, and the very idea of therapeutic abortion was considered an act of blasphemy, as it implied that the doctor knew better than God what should be done.

In contrast, Jewish law actually mandates abortion, if there is no other way to save the mother's life.

We value life, certainly. But we place the greatest value on existing life. If a mother loses a child in order to save her own life, she can always try again. If she dies, any future offspring die with her, and there's no guarantee that the baby will survive. By refusing to act, we can as easily throw away two lives instead of saving one.

Archbishop Lipscomb, in reprimanding Reverend Trosch, didn't take it all the way. He condemned Trosch's advocacy of killing abortionists, but reiterated the Church stand that abortion is, itself, a form of murder.

Still, it's a step above the Operation Rescue founder who praised the murder of Doctor Gunn in March.[8]

8   Doctor David Gunn, born 1946, was murdered on March 10, 1993 by Michael Griffin in Pensacola, Florida. Griffin was sentenced to life in prison a year later and as of 2011 is still serving his sentence.

There is a danger in fanaticism. If people become convinced that they're right, and everyone else is wrong, they tend to act on those beliefs. A fanatic might look at the story of Pinchas in the Torah, notice that he was singled out for special treatment after he killed Kosbi and Zimri, and argue that God allows inspired individuals to execute wrongdoers.

It just isn't so. The Torah mandates the establishment of courts, not individual justice. It is the community as a whole, not each person within it, that is given the task of establishing justice.

Even then, the community itself is often called to task. The prophets frequently spoke out against injustice perpetrated by the leaders of the people, or by the great majority of the people themselves.

Nor can we always accept the popular will as to what is right or wrong. The Michigan prosecutor who recently charged Kevorkian with assisting in a suicide has stated in print that he didn't really want to file the charges, since he doesn't see where anything wrong was actually done.

What is wrong, of course, is that the whole idea of allowing the terminally ill—or, in many cases, the terminally inconvenienced—to kill themselves tends, in time, to mutate into a societal mandate that these people commit suicide and stop wasting resources. Most countries with socialized medicine have incorporated death-by-neglect sentences into their laws. Most often based on age. In England, if you're over 60 and your kidneys fail, you don't get a new kidney and you don't get dialysis. You just die.

It's ethical only if you base your ethics 100% on cost.

When I was in Florida, where the average age of my congregants was, if anything, a little older than it is here, I spent a lot of time at the local hospitals. More than once, I encountered the children of elderly patients who had told their parents that they would "understand" if they chose not to endure any more pain. They wanted to be kind, to spare their mother or father the agony of final-stage cancer.

Except the patients—the parents—more than once asked me, "Rabbi, why do my children want me to kill myself? What did I do to make them hate me?"

And, more than once, I got the feeling that the real reason the children said they would "understand" if Mom or Dad took the easy way out had less to do with saving their parent from further pain, and a great deal to do with preserving that parent's assets for the children's benefit.

In every case where a patient *did* commit suicide, we had an "understanding" family. And, in every case where the spouse, or the children, made it clear to the patient that suicide was not an option, the patient stuck it out to the end. Or, in one case, made it through the worst and then got better.

The toughest patient I ever encountered was a man who had no family at all, and was determined to spend everything he had on his own care, just to insure that the state never got its hands on his money. He outlived his assets by about a week, as I recall.

Jewish law is fairy firm on these subjects. Abortion is permitted, or even mandatory, if the mother's life is in danger. We also permit it if there is a general danger to her health, whether physical or mental. Suicide is never permitted, with the exception of a handful of extremely rare circumstances that none of us here are ever likely to face.

So firmly is our tradition set against suicide that the very act is normally taken as conclusive evidence of insanity. A sane person would never kill himself, so anyone who does so has to be insane.[9]

Very often, it has been the task of Judaism as a whole to provide the moral center for society. This remains our task today. To remind the world that morality doesn't change just because proper behavior becomes inconvenient. To stand up and fight for what is right, even if it isn't popular.

To be, if we have to be, what we have always been. The conscience of the world.

---

[9] Psychiatric research has essentially borne out this ancient rabbinic conclusion. Successful suicides are nearly always found to have been suffering from clinical depression at the time they killed themselves.

D'var Torah: Shoftim

[August 21, 1993] Our Torah portion for this week is again taken from *Devarim* [*Deuteronomy*], beginning with Chapter 16, verse 18, and concluding with Chapter 21, verse 9. Our *sidrah* is called *Shoftim*, which is translated as "Judges," a title shared with the seventh book in the Hebrew canon.

Our *sidrah* begins: *Shoftim v'shotrim titein l'cha b'chol sha'arecha...* "Judges and [law] enforcing officers shall you appoint for yourselves in all your gates..." *Parashas Shoftim* begins, then, with the establishment of a judicial system for Israel, consisting of judges to decide the cases, and officers to enforce the law.

The *go'el ha'dam*, or "blood avenger," still exists even after these mandates are carried out, but his scope of action is significantly reduced. Justice is taken out of private hands and placed in those of the community.

Earlier, the Torah established the need for cities of refuge, where a person who was guilty of what we would today call manslaughter, or negligent homicide, could flee. In those cities the *go'el ha'dam* was forbidden to attack him.

One function of the courts was to determine if a killer was eligible for sanctuary. If the killing was ruled an accident, or unintentional, the killer was allowed to go to a city of refuge. If the killing was ruled deliberate — what we would today call first degree murder — no sanctuary was allowed. Such a murderer was to be taken even from the horns of the altar in the Temple and put to death.

A murderer was executed by beheading, and it was the duty of the *go'el ha'dam*, who would normally be a close relative of the victim, to act as executioner. Some have speculated that requiring a close relative of a murder victim, or the accuser in any other capital case, to be the executioner, or to throw the first stone, was a subtle way of reducing the number of executions.

Our sidrah is somewhat obsessed with the concept of justice. *Tzedek, tzedek tir'dof...* "Justice, justice, you shall pursue..." [*Deut.* 16:20]

And true justice, the Torah informs us, is even-handed. We are commanded not to favor the poor just because they are poor, nor to defer to the wealthy. In the eyes of the law, all are to be equal.

Here we also find the standard of evidence that is to be followed in any capital case: *Al pi sh'nayim eidim o sh'loshah eidim yumas ha'meis lo yumas al pi eid echad.* "On the word of two witnesses, or three witnesses, shall the condemned die, on the word of one witness he shall not be executed." [*Deut.* 17:6]

This is explicit. A single witness is never sufficient to establish guilt. Two are the minimum, more would be better.

In the United States, a similar rule applies to treason cases, which are the only category of crime actually defined in the body of the Constitution. Two witnesses are required for conviction, or a confession in open court.

Jewish law is stricter; confession is never allowed. In Jewish law, a man or woman can never condemn him or herself with their own words. Even if they admit the crime, their admission has to be disregarded, lest it prove to have been coerced, or be the result of delusion.

Jewish law differs in another way. A defendant cannot be charged with perjury. Perhaps the Torah simply presumes that a defendant is likely to lie in order to save himself. Besides, if confession is prohibited, a guilty defendant would have to lie, or else refuse to testify at all.

The penalty for perjury was reserved for witnesses *against* the accused: *Ki yakum eid chamas b'ish lei'einos bo sarah: V'am'du sh'nei ha'anashim asher lahem ha'riv lifnei HaShem lifnei ha'cohanim v'ha'shoftim asher yih'yu ba'yamim ha'hem: V'dar'shu ha'shoftim heiteiv v'hineh ad-sheker ha'eid sheker anah b'achiv: Va'asisem lo ka'asher zamam la'asos l'achaiv u'vi'arta ha'ra mik'r'beicha.* "If an evil witness arise against another man, to bear false witness against him, both men shall stand before the Lord, before the priests, and before the judges in those days. And the judges shall carefully inquire, and, see, if the witness is a false witness, and has testified falsely against his brother, then you shall do to him as he had tried to do to his brother. So shall you remove the evil from your midst." [*Deut.* 19:16-19]

That is, the penalty for perjury was the same as the penalty for the crime the accused was charged with. If the penalty was a fine, the false witness was fined the same amount. If the penalty was death, the false witness was executed. This may sound a little harsh as a penalty for lying, but the lies were intended to trick the court into committing murder.

Our *sidrah* continues on this subject: *V'lo sachos ein-eicha, nefesh b'nefesh, ayin b'ayin, shein b'shein, yad b'yad, regel b'regel.* "Have no pity in your eyes: life for life, eye for eye, tooth for tooth, hand for hand, foot for foot." [*Deut.* 19:21]

The Sages teach us, however, that only the first of these, "life for life," was ever intended to be taken literally. All of the others are to be read as "the *value* of an eye for an eye," and so on. That a murderer was to be executed was simply logical. But for any sort of maiming, accidental or intentional, exact equivalency is virtually impossible. And what, the Rabbis asked, if a man who is already blind causes a sighted man to lose an eye? Removing the blind man's eye doesn't change his condition at all, and so is clearly not a punishment. Since it is necessary that the punishment be equal, it follows that monetary compensation must be intended.

The *haftarah* for this morning is the fourth of the seven *haftaros* of consolation, and consists of *Isaiah* 51:12 through 52:12. Here, God is portrayed as one who consoles Israel, and will return her to her land when the time of her punishment is ended.

Shoot the Doctor

[August 27, 1993] I wrote a sermon for last week but, as we were more or less rained out, and the topic remains interesting, I'll give you a slightly modified version of it tonight.

As of last Friday, Doctor Kevorkian had been arrested for helping a young man kill himself; a woman had been arrested after attempting to murder an obstetrician who was also providing abortion services; and a Catholic priest in Alabama had been reprimanded for suggesting that it would be perfectly okay for good Christians to kill any doctors who were performing abortions.

There is a curious logic in all of this. On the one hand, we have people shooting doctors who perform abortions, in which, at least from our point of view, no actual human being is killed. On the other hand, over in Michigan, we have a doctor who is helping mentally ill people commit an inherently irrational act by taking their own lives, who definitely *is* killing people.

The two people who have actually killed one abortion provider, and attempted to kill another, both argue that their actions are justified. They claim, in fact, that by killing these physicians, they are saving thousands of lives. By their lights, any doctor who performs abortions, for any reason, is a murderer and deserves to be executed. Since the government isn't going to do this, they take it upon themselves.

Part of this is clearly religious. Particularly on the part of the priest who was advocating killing doctors. The Catholic Church never permits abortion, under any circumstances. A standard Catholic medical ethics text, published at a time when the law in all state forbade abortion except to save the mother's life, decreed that even *this* was forbidden. The author argued that it was up to God to decide whether the mother or the baby, or both, or neither, would survive. This remains Catholic doctrine to this day.

Jewish law looks at this differently. The *halakha* does not consider an unborn child to be a person. Rather, the fetus is looked upon as an appendage of the mother. Thus, just as we would allow amputation of a gangrenous arm in order to save a life, so we allow abortion if continuing the pregnancy will endanger the mother's life.

In ancient times, this permission existed right up until the moment of birth. It was only after the head had been delivered that the child was considered a separate individual, whose life was, from that moment, of equal importance with its mother. If delivery was impossible — such as when the mother's pelvic opening is too small to allow the baby's head to pass through — the Talmud permitted the baby to be killed in the womb and dissected, so that it could be delivered in pieces. This was justified under the doctrine of the *rodef*, one who pursues a person with the intention of causing their death. Since the delivery will kill the mother, the unborn baby is considered to fit this definition.

Today, of course, this sort of thing almost never actually happens, since modern medical science allows the performance of a Caesarian section in these cases. In

Talmudic times, a C-section was strictly an emergency procedure, performed only on a dead mother.

Now, we might note that when Archbishop Lipscomb reprimanded Reverend Trosch for suggesting that abortionists be killed, he didn't say that he was approving of abortion. He simply took the same tack that the Church takes on abortion itself. It was up to God to decide who should die, and mere mortals shouldn't try to make such decisions. Two wrongs, in other words, still don't make a right.

The truth is, no branch of Judaism give blanket approval to abortion. But we do place the health of the mother, both physical and mental, above the potential for life of the fetus. Traditionally, we have felt that the soul entered the body not at conception, as in Catholic theology, but with the first breath following birth. Our tradition even suggests that the soul is not firmly attached to the body until 30 days after birth. Hence, we do not require that a formal funeral service be held if an infant dies in the first 30 days. (Though, in most cases today, a funeral is still likely to be held, as it allows a mechanism for the parents to grieve.)

Now, if we accept the possibility of abortion under somewhat limited conditions—and object strenuously to any governmental bar that would restrict this possibility—our position on suicide is much more clear cut.

People like Kevorkian try to distinguish between suicide in healthy people, which they consider a sign of mental illness, and suicide by the terminally ill, which they think is just an alternative way of going out.[10] And,

---

10   In retrospect, Kevorkian may not have cared that much about the distinction. A relatively large group of his "patients" turned out to not actually have been terminal, and several were not even sick. He never was convicted on an assisted suicide charge. His 1998 conviction came when it was found that he had not assisted at a suicide, but had actually killed the patient him-

in fact, many people agree with this. The prosecutor in Michigan charged with the current Kevorkian case has publicly expressed his reluctance to prosecute, as he personally disagrees with the law on assisted suicide.

The greatest danger in allowing terminally ill patients to simply kill themselves is that what is "allowed" often turns into what is "required." When it becomes inconvenient to care for a patient, why not suggest they kill themselves? Or, even better, why not just kill them? Give them an overdose. Or just don't bother to treat them.

Many of the countries we are studying as possible models for universal medical care incorporate just such "death by neglect" provisions in their laws. England and Canada both set age limits for some procedures. If you live in England, and your kidneys stop working, you'd better be younger than 60 or you won't be eligible for a transplant and, even worse, you won't get dialysis, either. Some bureaucrat has decided that these resources should be allocated to younger people, who, presumably, will have more time left to contribute to society.

This, of course, is the sort of logic that presumes that a 23-year-old pickpocket is more likely to benefit society than a 72-year-old physicist who was just nominated for his second Nobel Prize. This may seem cost effective to someone running a socialized medical system, but it really isn't very ethical.

And neither is suggesting that terminally ill people kill themselves and stop bothering people.

I ran across a few cases of elderly people killing themselves when I was in Florida. None of them did it to avoid pain. They did it to please their children. Because, when a child says to his mother, "Mom, you're in pain, and I'd understand if you killed yourself," what

---

self, even if it was at the victim's direction.

Mom really hears is, "You're wasting money I should be inheriting, so will you please kill yourself and quit bothering everyone." I never saw a suicide in a terminal patient where there wasn't an "understanding" family to encourage them.

On the other hand, in every case where the family made it clear that suicide was *not* acceptable, the patient fought it out to the end.

Jewish law considers suicide inherently insane. We forbid a funeral for a suicide, but then define it in such a way that only one of 500 is ruled a true suicide. The rest are deaths while insane. And psychology backs this up, having noticed that clinical depression is an inevitable ingredient in nearly all suicides.

This is one of those places where we, as Jews, are called upon to demonstrate moral and ethical leadership, even if popular opinion seems to be against us. If Kevorkian advocates suicide, it is our duty to oppose him. To make people recognize that what is popular, or "easy," isn't always right.

To be, as we have always been, the conscience of the world.

Content or *Kavanah*?

[August 31, 1993] When we *daven*, there is always a conflict in every congregation. It is a conflict which inevitably exists in every *minyan*. Certain members are clock-conscious. Others are more concerned with *kavanah*—with the meaning and intent of the prayers.

When I was on vacation, the cantor at the *shul* I attended in Cleveland commented to me that he expected some of the people at the services to raise a complaint, since it finished at four minutes past noon. And he wondered at the justice of this, as they had added *Anim Z'miros* to the preliminary service that morning, after having left it out for the last several years.

The preliminary services, he said, were about 15 minutes long when he started at the *shul*, and now had grown to 38 minutes. But they were still starting at exactly 9:00 am, so why did people expect them to *end* at he same time?

Now, I might mention, the Cleveland congregation takes a more leisurely approach to their services than we do. Even in the daily services, speed isn't considered a primary factor. They begin their weekday morning service at 7:30, just as we do, but, while we're usually finished by about 7:55—or 8:05, if it's a Monday or Thursday and we read the Torah—they finish up at about 8:45.

Okay, the main reason we rush through the services on weekdays is for the benefit of those who need to get to work. But what about *shabbos?* We call this a Conservative congregation, and Conservative tradition is exactly the same as Orthodox when it comes to working on *shabbos.* We may do so only if our profession involves saving lives.

It has been argued that Conservative Judaism tends to let everyone do whatever they wish. But that isn't true. Conservative Jews are bound by the *halakha,* and differ from Orthodox Jews mainly in the interpretation. There are certain things we are required to do. And there are certain things we are not supposed to do.

On *shabbos,* for instance, we are not allowed to drive or ride in an automobile, except for the purpose of driving to *shul* and directly home again, and only if it's too far to walk. We are not allowed to work at a job that doesn't involve saving human lives or, at least, involves the potential of doing so, such as working as a police officer or fireman.

We are not allowed to turn on a television or radio, or listen to the stereo, unless the program we're watching or listening to has a clear Jewish religious theme. We're not supposed to cook, though we permit warming previously cooked foods.

What this adds up to is the question, why, on *shabbos,* are we in such a hurry to get out of the *shul?* Our services last, on average, about an hour and 50 minutes. We rarely repeat either the *shachris* or *musaf amidah* and, while we read the full *haftarah,* the Torah reading is usually quite short even for a triennial cycle. In most Conservative congregations, *shabbos* morning services run an average of three hours, or a bit more. Orthodox services often run about four hours.

True, most are still finished about noon. They simply start earlier than we do. And there is always the question, are we really getting everything we need out of this? Are we more concerned with the style and *nusach*, or is our primary concern the *kavanah*?

Well, perhaps we can take a closer look at this after the holidays, as the next couple of Tuesdays will be taken up with preparing for Rosh Ha'Shanah and Yom Kippur.

Jewish Thinking

[September 3, 1993] I noticed an interesting letter in one of the newspapers I subscribe to this past week. The letters are always interesting. There's one fellow who's always complaining that the whole Reform movement is being betrayed because most of today's Reform rabbis wear *yarmulkes,* use *chassidic* and Israeli melodies for certain prayers, and generally run services that the average synagogue visitor would immediately think looked Jewish rather than, say, Presbyterian.

There's another letter writer who's always complaining about the first writer, reminding him that there's nothing wrong with acting Jewish if that's what you happen to be.

There are different sorts of Judaism. There's the sort that comes from having a Jewish mother. It's official, sure, but it doesn't really mean very much if that's all you have. In fact, if this Jewish identity through parentage is never more than that, it means nothing at all, since the child, though Jewish, doesn't identify with it.

Biology has a place in Jewish identity. But it isn't always as powerful a place as many like to think. Edith Stein was Jewish by birth, and died in Auschwitz because of that. But she died there declaring that the Holocaust was a just punishment for the stubbornness of the Jewish people, and this was all the more bitter to her because, after all, she thought she had left that Jewish taint behind when she became a nun.

At last report, she was well on her way to becoming a Roman Catholic saint.[11]

To be Jewish really involves more than simple biology. It's also a way of thinking. And this is what that latter writer I mentioned was getting at. He was a rabbi, and he was saying that, while rabbis and other Jewish professionals have a place in Jewish education, maybe it was time to quit blaming the rabbi, or the school principal, if your child runs off and marries a Methodist.

The emphasis in this whole area has often been wrongly placed. An old favorite was guilt. Marry a non-Jew, and you're betraying everyone who died in the Holocaust. Or, another favorite, "For all these generations, all of your ancestors resisted assimilation, and now you're going to betray that heritage."

The problem with the first is that, today, too many young people—even Jewish young people—really have no concept of what the Holocaust was. The percentage of Americans under 25 who question whether there even *was* a Holocaust is a little frightening. And, even when our young people have been taught the facts, and understand the truth, they find it difficult to see how their choice of a marriage partner is going to make things any better or worse.

The second argument is even worse. Because the truth is, if all of that child's ancestors really *had* resisted assimilation, the world Jewish population today would be around 3 to 400-million. It obvious isn't, though there are certainly that many people walking around on

---

11   Stein was canonized in 1998. She is claimed as both a German and Polish saint, having been born in Breslau, which was in the part of Germany taken over by Poland at the end of World War II.

this planet who are descended from Jews if you just go back far enough. The kid's direct ancestors may have resisted, but a lot of others didn't.

And, as for blaming the rabbi, or the school... Well, it makes just as much sense to blame to parents. When our children come to religious school, they are taught a little Hebrew, and they're taught quite a bit of ritual. Particularly home ritual. How to light candles. The proper blessings for various foods. When to say the *birchas ha'mazon*, and which forms to use, depending upon how many people are at the table, and what day of the week it happens to be. They're taught how to observe *shabbos*, what we're permitted to do, and what we're not.

And then they go home, and notice that their parents, who are both Jewish, don't actually do any of these things. That Judaism is, to their parents, more of an ethnic identity, with very little spiritual content. Something that just isn't very important, except maybe around *Pesach*, or on Yom Kippur.

Can we blame these children for being surprised when Mom and Dad suddenly turn into passionate Jews when the child brings home a Baptist and announces that a wedding is planned? No matter what they may have learned in their religious school, their home environment made it clear that no one was taking any of this too seriously. Or so it seemed.

What is needed may be a different sort of education. Not just in prayers and ritual and language, but in a way of thinking. We need to teach our children to think as Jews. And not only our children, but also ourselves.

Is our ordinary language Jewish? What do you exclaim when someone cuts you off at a corner and nearly causes a wreck? Do you yell, *"Oy! Gevalt!"* Or do you mention the name of the founder of another religion?

What day is tomorrow? Is it *shabbos?* Or is it just Saturday?

What's the difference, you might ask? Well, simply put, people work on Saturday, but *shabbos* is holy to our people, and on a metaphysical level transcends all other days of the week. *Shabbos* is the reason we exist. It reminds us of where we come from. It reminds us of who created the universe we live in, and of the wonder of our very existence. It reminds us that we were slaves in Egypt, brought forth from bondage in fulfillment of a promise made by God to Abraham. It reminds us that, on this one day, our Creator has freed us from the constant toil which is our lot, and elevated us to a higher plane and freed us to rest. Just as he rested after finishing the work of creation.

Saturday, on the other hand, is just another day.

We need to make our thinking more Jewish. We need to feel that, for instance, marrying a non-Jew would be a betrayal, not of our ancestors, or of Holocaust victims, or of our parents rarely-expressed feelings, but of ourselves. That we would be denying ourselves a lifetime of sharing what is most central in our lives.

The best defense against assimilation into the surrounding culture is a stubborn resolve to make our very thought processes thoroughly Jewish. To purge foreign religious references from our vocabularies. To make what is central to our faith also central to ourselves.

As we approach the *Yomim Noraim*, we turn our thoughts inward. What do we find? Do we find Jews? Jews who think as Jews, and act as Jews? Or do we find people who only call themselves Jews in the synagogue, and do a pretty good job of hiding it the rest of the time?

It's something we need to ask ourselves.

First Evening
Rosh Ha'Shanah 5754

[September 15, 1993] Here we are, once again, at the beginning of another year. At the start of each year, I like to see if I can work a little *gematria* with the date. You see, Hebrew, unlike English, uses the letter of the alphabet not only as letters, but also as numbers. Consequently, the year frequently spells something, and often we can find a significance — or, at least, a theme — in this.

Now so far in this decade what the years have spelled is nothing. They're not forming words. But a couple of days ago I was playing with some of the other numbers. If we take the date 27 Elul 5753, and we add the numbers of the date, together with the numerical value of Elul, which is 61, we get a total of 5,841. Adding these digits together, we have a total of 18 and, by adding the 8 and the 1, our final total is 9.

If we then take the numerical value of the word *shalom*, which is 936, we find that those digits also add up to 18 and may be reduced to 9. So the numerical value of 27 Elul 5753 is the same as the numerical value of *shalom*.

For anyone who hasn't figured it out yet, 27 Elul 5753 was Monday, when a preliminary peace agreement was signed between Israel and the PLO.

Perhaps also significantly, before we reduce them to a single digit, both the date and *shalom* are *shemoneh asar*, which spelled backwards is *chai*, or "life." Thus, by this *gematria*, we find hope that this accord may actually achieve peace, and result in a new hope for life for our people.[12]

Our Sages taught that peace for Israel is also peace for all of humanity. As the people through whom God would teach his laws to the rest of the world, Israel has a special place in the scheme of things. We have been told, *Ki mi tzion tetze torah, u'd'var HaShem mi'y'rushalayim.* "From Zion shall go forth Torah, and the word of the Lord from Jerusalem."

When Israel is persecuted, the rest of the world also suffers. The persecutor is reduced in stature. He becomes less of a person.

Jewish tradition speaks of 36 *tzaddikim.* Thirty-six totally righteous individuals, on whose collective merit the world is permitted to continue to exist. And, while we tend to presume that the 36 are Jews, we really don't know. But we can say with absolute assurance that at least one of them must be, for if a time ever comes when the last Jew dies, or converts to another faith, our Sages tell us that the world will end at that very moment. So that last Jew would seem certain to be one of the 36, who through his death removes not only the Jewish people from this earth, but also the Jewish presence that allows the rest of humanity to exist.

So peace would seem to be a good thing. If Israel

---

12   Jews are, if nothing else, eternally optimistic. As we now know, this peace accord worked out about as well as any of the others, which is not well at all. It would no doubt help if the Arab side started viewing peace as the object, and not as a rest period before resuming their goal of removing Israel from the map and returning it to its old status as an Arab colony.

doesn't have to fight with her neighbors, her people may finally be allowed to generally live out their normal spans. An Israel where Yeshiva students can walk home from their studies without having to worry about being stabbed and murdered for the crime of being visibly Jewish is something we can all hope for.

Golda Meier, some years ago, was asked if she hated the Arabs for killing Israel's sons. She answered, "No—but I cannot forgive them for making our sons kill theirs."

Unique among the nations of the world, Israel has never expressed an interest in expanding beyond the borders set down in the Torah. True, these borders are somewhat more extensive than Israel's current territory, but even modern Israel has shown no urges toward expansion. What territory has been added was the result of attacks by Israel's neighbors, who were punished for their aggression by the loss of their land.

So, will there be peace in this new year? The letters used to write 5754, *tav, shin, nun,* and *dales,* add up to 16, which may be reduced to 7. Since there are six days in the week, along with the seventh, *shabbos,* six and one equals seven can also be said to equal *shabbos.* And what is a prime characteristic of *shabbos,* if not *m'nuchah,* or "rest," the most important prerequisite for which is peace? *Shalom.*

We might even note that 5754 is also a seventh year. A year of *shemittah,* on which the land of Israel itself is to be afforded a year long sabbath. Nothing will be planted, and nothing will be harvested. Whatever grows of its own accord is common property, and anyone may pick enough for his or her own immediate needs.

In our tradition, during the *shemittah* year, the farmer is to become like the scholar and devote himself to Torah study. The leisure time should not be spent in idleness, but in adding to the store of human knowledge and understanding.

Our *sidrah* for last week reminded us that Torah study is not something which is beyond our capabilities. Our neighbors instituted an entirely new religion, declaring that the Torah was too difficult to understand, and its laws too numerous to be obeyed. That it provided an impossible standard, and that no one could follow it without sinning.

Perhaps.

What is a sin, after all, but a failure to achieve the standard set out for us? Does failing to accomplish something on the first try mean that it's impossible? When I was 16, I failed my first driving test. But I have a license now, and have had one for 28 years. If you fail a driving test, you don't immediately conclude that it's impossible to pass, and that you're going to have to settle for taking the bus. You study some more, and then you take the test again. And you keep taking it until you pass.

And sin is like that. If we fail once, we cannot presume that we will always fail. If you find yourself walking into a McDonalds and eating a Big Mac, must you then conclude that you will be forever incapable of eating properly? Or do you look at the wrapper after you've eaten and say, "This is wrong, this is *treif,* and I'm going to have to control my urges more carefully in the future?" The very fact that you have that little twinge of guilt as you consume your cheeseburger is a sign that there's still hope.

Tonight begins Rosh Ha'Shanah. The head of the year. Not the new year, really, but its head. And the Rosh Ha'Shanah should remind you of the *rosh ha'adam*—the human head. Of which we all have one.

What do we use our heads for? A convenient place to put a *yarmulke?* A place to rest half a set of *t'fillin?* A container for our brain?

We think with our brains. Decartes held that thinking was what made us human. That, if we didn't think, we would not exist.

The Torah declares that we were created *b'tzelelim Elokim,* in the image of God. By this, our Sages taught, it was meant that, like God, we had the ability to know good from evil. That we could choose right from wrong. That we had free will.

If we can choose to do wrong, we can also choose to do what is right. On Rosh Ha'Shanah we must use our own *rosh,* our own head, and think back over the past year. Discover where we have failed to live up to the standard our Torah has set for us. And we have to make a conscious decision to change.

If the standards we set for ourselves have been too low, then we must decided to change them. The Hebrew word for repentance, *t'shuvah,* actually means "to turn." To turn from what is wrong toward what is right. To change paths.

If we are on the wrong path, then we are moving away from God. So we must turn in *t'shuvah* and return to him.

An old *midrash* spoke of a man who was a constant sinner. Each time he would sin, he would immediately regret it, and he would beg God to forgive him, to give him another chance. After this had happened many times, one of the angels asked our Creator, "This man is always sinning, and always asking to be forgiven, and you always forgive. How many times must you forgive such a person?"

And God answered, "We are required to forgive exactly one more time than we are asked."

"On Rosh Ha'Shanah it is written, on Yom Kippur it is sealed." We have ten days to get our lives in order. To make whatever changes need to be made. We are never so lost that God cannot find us and bring us back, so long as we make a sincere effort to return to him.

First Morning
Rosh Ha'Shanah 5754

[September 16, 1993] The Torah portion we read this morning begins with the words, *V'HaShem pachad es Sarah, ka'asher amar, va'ya'as HaShem l'Sarah ka'asher dibeir.* "And the Lord remembered Sarah, as he had said, and the Lord did to Sarah as he had said." [Gen. 21:1]

What God remembered was his promise that Sarah should bear a child in her old age. Because he remembered this, Sarah gave birth to Yitz'chak, who was to carry on the line of his father Avraham and be, in turn, the father of Ya'akov, who would later be given the name of Yisroel.

In our *haftarah*, too, we find the theme of birth. Channah was sad because she had given her husband no children, but when she poured out her sorrow before God at Shiloh, her prayer was answered, and she later gave birth to Sh'muel. In the same morning, we find commemorated the birth of the second of the patriarchs, and the last of the judges.

On Rosh Ha'Shanah, the themes of birth, and of remembrance, become very appropriate. The one advantage a newborn infant has over an adult is that the child has no sins to account for. Each morning, in our prayers, we proclaim a basic truth, *Elokai n'shamah she'nasata bi t'horah hi*. "My God, the soul you have given to me is pure."

An infant, unlike an adult, is incapable of sinning. Our tradition teaches that sin requires consciousness. If you do not know that what you are doing is wrong, you cannot be held accountable for it. As Jews, we are bound by a great many *mitzvos*, or commandments. Most of us are actually aware of only a small percentage of them.

A Jew who has never learned that it is wrong to eat shrimp or lobster will not be punished for doing so. But from the moment he learns of this law, he may expect to be punished if he continues. Moreover, in the time when the Temple still stood in Jerusalem, he would have been required to bring a sin offering to be sacrificed. And this responsibility would begin at the moment he was informed of his error.

A child, who may have heard of a particular *mitzvah*, will not be held responsible for violating it unless he is not only aware of the rule in a general way, but actually understands what it implies. Until that time, his parents are responsible for his transgressions. There is even a special prayer, which the father says at a *bar mitzvah*, which thanks God for relieving him of the responsibility for his son's sins.

But most of us aren't children. And most of us are only too aware of our failings. We know we are far from perfect. We know, deep down, that we have never quite become the person we really wanted to be. There is always something we could do better. There is always some fault in our character we wish to correct.

And now, on Rosh Ha'Shanah, we're given another chance. It is said that, on this day, God opens three books, and writes the name of every person in one of them. Those who are hopelessly evil, and incapable of redemption, are written in the book of death, and will inevitably die before another year has passed. Those who are completely good, the true *tzaddikim*, are written in the book of life, and will certainly see the start of next year.

But most of us, who are neither all good nor all bad, will be written in a book titled "Undecided." The final judgment is deferred, and our fate remains undecided until Yom Kippur.

What we often fail to realize, however, is that most human beings are capable of repentance. People can change. How many of us, after all, still hold exactly the same opinions on every subject that we held when we finished high school? How many, for that matter, haven't changed our minds on something as recently as the last couple of weeks?

We're Jews. We are inherently optimistic. If we weren't, how can we account for our continued existence after nearly twenty centuries of persecution? No matter how dark things may be, we look forward to a future when they will be better.

Other cultures look backwards, to a golden age in the long ago past. Greeks speak of Plato and Aristotle, of Pythagoras and Socrates. Italians look back with great pride to the glories of ancient Rome. The British remember more recent glories, when the sun never set on their empire.

Not us. We remember ancient Israel, to be sure. But even in ancient times, our sights were set on the future. We didn't look back to past glories, but always looked hopefully forward to a future messianic age, when all humanity would at last come to recognize the truths we had been teaching for all these centuries.

We see a world, bad as it is, which is capable of changing for the better. And we see human beings in the same light. No one, it seems, is really so evil that they cannot change. There is a former Klan leader who so thoroughly repented his past hatreds that he converted to Judaism a few years ago, and now directs his efforts toward educating the current crop of bigots on the errors of their beliefs.

Now if someone like that can change, there is surely hope for the rest of us. In this season, these ten days between Rosh Ha'Shanah and Yom Kippur, we are given every opportunity to become better people. Even if we have been written down as subject to a harsh decree, there is still time to repent and turn our lives around.

On this day, we acknowledge that we are only mortal beings and, as such, capable of error. The *chazzan* will begin the *musaf* service with the chanting of *Hineni*. "Here I am, come to offer prayers for Israel before you, O God, and yet I am no more than a sinner myself. Unworthy. Hear my prayers on behalf of the congregation, and do not be swayed against them because of my own failings."

A *chazzan*, or anyone who leads a service, is the *shaliach tzibbur*. The emissary of the congregation. He is a part of the congregation, to be sure, but his words carry a special significance, for he prays not only for himself, but also for all those who lack the ability. When he repeats the *amidah*, his words become the words of all who answer each blessing with "amen."

But the composer of this prayer, this *Hineni*, was unsure of his own merits. Humble, and yet, perhaps, fearful that even his humility was false. Perhaps he was humble because it was expected that he should be, when he didn't feel that way at all. And so he prayed that his own faults should not condemn those on whose behalf his prayers were offered.

And in each congregation, to this day, the *chazzan*

invokes the same prayer. "If I am unworthy, do not condemn these others in my place."

Between now and Yom Kippur we have ten days. Use them to look deep within yourself. Examine your deeds, and if you have harmed someone, seek their forgiveness. And, if you're asked to forgive, do so. Don't let vindictiveness at the slights of others turn into an added measure of sin for yourself.

When we sin we are moving away from God. *T'shuvah*—repentance—means turning back toward him.

It's something we are all capable of doing.

Second Evening
Rosh Ha'Shanah 5754

[September 16, 1993] Rosh Ha'Shanah is unique. Because of ancient problems with our calendar, most festivals are observed for a single day in *Eretz Yisroel*, and for two days in the diaspora. This is because, many years ago, the first day of the month was determined by direct observation of the first sliver of the new moon.

In Israel, it was possible to get the news to the entire country within a day or two. It's a small country. And, since most of the festivals begin around the time of the full moon, on the 14th or 15th of the month, everyone knew the proper date.

Outside of Israel, however, communication was slower, so the messengers didn't always arrive in time. For a time a signaling system was employed, using bonfires on hilltops. But this proved impractical, because the Samaritans, who took considerable pleasure in making things difficult for Jews, did their best to sabotage the system by lighting false signal fires.

With the only other practical system being the use of messengers who might, or might not, reach outlying settlements in time, an alternative system developed. Because the date of the previous new moon was always known, it became the custom to start the new month on the most probable day, but to add an extra day to each festival, just in case the month had been started a day early.

That system, somewhat modified, continues even today, though we've had a reliable calendar since the 4th century, when Hillel II published the rules for regulating it. When we start a festival today, we can be certain that the date is correct. We retain the second day based on the principle, "We follow the custom of our ancestors."

But Rosh Ha'Shanah was different. Unlike the other festivals, Rosh Ha'Shanah falls *on* Rosh Chodesh. Even in Jerusalem there wasn't time for witnesses to see the first sliver of new moon, and the Sanhedrin to declare the new month. The services had to start at sunset, before the moon appeared.

For this reason, it was decided to begin the services on the first of the two possible nights on which the new moon might appear. If it did not appear, it was certain to appear the next night, and the observance was carried over. If the new moon appeared the first night, the observance ended with a single day.

When there were two days, the Sages taught, they were considered as being a single long day.

Curiously, Rosh Ha'Shanah represents the only instance of a diaspora custom being imported to *Eretz Yisroel* and displacing the original Israeli custom. With Hillel's calendar, Israel observed only one day of Rosh Ha'Shanah. European Jews moving to Israel in the Middle Ages brought back the European custom of a two-day Rosh Ha'Shanah and it took hold.

In a modern sidelight to this, Conservative and Orthodox congregations in the United States have always observed two days of Rosh Ha'Shanah, while

Reform congregations generally observed only one. Today, there is a growing trend for Reform congregations to observe two day—possibly because the Reform *machsor* contains two separate services for Rosh Ha'Shanah—while a number of Conservative congregations have recently been experimenting with a single day observance.

This afternoon, we observed the *taschlich* ritual.[13] Someone once remarked that is potentially a very expensive ritual, since the *halakha* is not actually to empty merely the symbolic break crumbs from our pockets, but to empty *everything* from them. Since this is done on the afternoon of the first day of Rosh Ha'Shanah, when we are forbidden to carry anything from one domain to another, this represents no potential for loss for a traditional Jew. His pockets are going to be empty in any case.

On the other hand, strictly speaking, if you have your wallet, house keys, comb, and appointment book in your pockets, you're supposed to throw *them* into the water, too.

Well, *halakhic* anecdotes aside, why do we even do this? In ancient times, on Yom Kippur, we observed the ritual of the scapegoat, in which the sins of the entire nation were placed on the head of a goat, which was then sent out into the wilderness. If the goat didn't return to the city, it was held that the sins had been forgiven. If the goat came back, it was presumed there would be problems (which was why the goat was usually led out of the city and pushed off a cliff). This was a casting away of sins in a vividly symbolic manner.

In the same way, the more modern *kapores* ritual, in

---

13 Actually, I don't remember if we did this or not, as it would have depended on the weather. The typed sermon, done several days in advance, was written to cover either alternative.

which a live hen or rooster is waved over one's head, symbolically removing our sins, is a vivid ritual. One which has, by the way, remained popular even in the face of several centuries of rabbinic condemnation.

But what about *tashlich?* Is this another symbolic gesture? We say that the crumbs in our pockets represent our sins, which we symbolically cast into the water. It provides a visible sign, representing the internal purging of our sins that we are commanded to make at this time of year. We often find it easier to visualize when there is a concrete action involved.

This is what we have to do now. Because the symbolic action involved in *tashlich* is by far secondary to the true need for repentance. For *t'shuvah*.

We all make mistakes. We all fail to live up to the standards expected of us.

And each year, our Creator gives us another chance. If we can recognize our faults, and make a sincere effort to correct them, we may be afforded another year of life. Our Sages taught that death comes only from sin, though, it must be pointed out, not always our own. The good who seem to unfairly suffer may be atoning for the errors of an evil ancestor, and the evil who seem unjustly rewarded may be reaping the benefits of an exemplary grandparent.

And, we must remember, some will be set down in the book of death not because their deeds in the last year are deserving of that fate, but simply because their allotted time has run out.

For if death comes only through sin, we must remember that this is cumulative. Joseph was sentenced to die ten years before the Biblical ideal of 120 because of the ten times he permitted his brothers to refer to his father as his servant. When we slander someone, a span of minutes, or hours, or weeks, or even months may be subtracted from our allotment. That shrimp dinner at Red Lobster may cost us an hour of life. That lustful desire for someone else's wife—covetousness being the only one of the commandments that may be violated by simply thinking—may be good for ten minutes less life.

Yet sincere repentance may erase these forfeitures. If we sin against God, he is always willing to forgive. If we sin against another person, we can always ask them to be forgiven. And if we are asked for forgive, we should do so, for a stubborn refusal to forgive another's misdeeds is considered equally a sin.

We are who we are. But we all have the potential to be better.

And now is the time to make the effort.

Second Morning Rosh Ha'Shanah 5754

[September 17, 1993] The story found in our Torah reading for this second morning of Rosh Ha'Shanah is one of the most familiar in scripture. And it has provided a challenge to generations of rabbis, for this story is so firmly implanted in our tradition that it would be considered close to heresy to talk about anything else.

It is also a story which seems frequently to be misunderstood.

The story is the *akeidah*, commonly called in English, the binding of Isaac. We've just read it, so I'll give only a brief outline. Abraham is to be put to a test. Take Isaac to the mountains of Moriah, and sacrifice him there. Abraham does as he is told, and at the last instant God stops him, providing a ram as a substitute.

What can we learn from this? First, that a willingness to sacrifice is often all that is really required. Abraham was willing to give up the one thing he loved the most. More, he was willing to lose his posterity. Sarah was already 137 years old. For her to have a second son might well require more than just a simple miracle.

And Isaac, too, was willing. In the *Midrash*, we find the story of why he was bound before being placed on the altar. It was Isaac's idea. He preferred to be tied securely, for he feared he might flinch at the last moment, causing the knife to slip and the sacrifice to be ruined.

The Torah called Isaac *na'ar,* or "lad." Yet it is firmly established in our tradition that he was a "lad" only compared to his father, who was nearly to the mid-point of his second century. Isaac was, we are told, what today we would surely consider middle-aged, a man of 47.

So both father and son were willing to participate in this sacrifice, even though both certainly considered it an extreme test, and no doubt wondered how it could be in their own interests. God had promised that Abraham should grow into a great nation through the offspring of Isaac, yet, at this time, he had yet to marry. How could he then be sacrificed, if he was also to produce children?

It has been suggested that, from the start, Abraham never truly believed that he would actually have to kill his son. As the pair started up the mountain path, he told those he left at the bottom, *Sh'vu lachem poh, im ha'chamor, v'ani v'ha'na'ar nel'chah ad ko, v'nish'tachaveh, v'n'shuvah aleichem.* "Stay here with the donkey, and the lad and I will go over there and worship, and then come back to you."

Rashi comments on this passage, *nis'na'beh she'ya'shuvu sh'neihem.* "He prophesized that both would return."

Rashi further noted, after Isaac was taken down from the makeshift altar unharmed, *Amar lo HaKadosh, baruch hu, lo achalel b'risi, u'motza s'fasai lo ashaneh—lo amarti l'cha sh'chateihu eleh; ha'allehu, asak'tei, acha'tei.* "The Holy One, blessed be he, said to him, I shall not profane my covenant, and the utterance of my lips shall not change. When I said to you, 'take,' I did not say to you, 'slay him,' but 'lift him up.' You have lifted him up, now bring him down."

This section has been interpreted as refuting one of the arguments our neighbors have used for centuries in an attempt to convince us that we're obsolete. Blood sacrifice is not the only means of atonement. Rashi declares that Abraham's intentions were all that were required. And, in this brief story, we are reminded that God made it clear from the very beginning of our history that human sacrifice would not be acceptable. If those we live amidst wish to base their faith on the necessity of human sacrifice, we must be able to rise to greater spiritual heights.

For some 4,000 years our people have done their best to set an example of righteous living for those around us. We haven't always accomplished this goal, but our failures should always be seen in a positive light. Even when we fail, we are still trying. You can easily live a life in which you will never fail, but only if you also never try.

You can't fail if you don't try. But you won't accomplish anything, either.

And we need, sometimes, a little faith. We need to believe. The closest thing Judaism has to a creed is the declaration, twice each day, *Sh'ma Yisroel, HaShem elokeinu, HaShem echad.* "Hear, O Israel, HaShem is our God, HaShem is One." And, having made this declaration, we are reminded of our duties to our Creator, and of what he will do for us if we obey his laws, and also what he will do *to* us if we don't.

To modern Jews, the very real need to believe that God is God, and that he makes demands upon us as Jews, often seems a little quaint. Our faith, after all, is based on the performance of *mitzvos.* On action. It's our neighbors who have always espoused the idea that it really doesn't matter what you do, as long as you believe the right way.

We would never put forward such an idea. Faith has meaning only when it is expressed in action. It isn't enough just to believe in God. We are also required to carry out his commandments. To participate in the ancient imperative of *tikkun olam*. Of repairing the world.

God deliberately left off the act of creation a bit short of perfection, and gave the responsibility of completing the world to us. In the same way, he deliberately sends each male human being into the world not quite finished, giving us the *mitzvah* of *b'ris millah,* and of training *mohelim* to complete the work.

If we have to finish the work of completing our sons' bodies—girls apparently come already perfect—are we not also required to finish the world?

Our tradition teaches us that Moshiach will come in one of two ways. If the world is ready, and deserving of miracles, he will come in a miraculous manner. But if the world is not deserving of miracles, he will come in an ordinary way. Through the normal workings of human society.

In the *Zohar*, we find a prediction that the beginning of the coming of *Moshiach* will occur in the middle of the 19th century of the Common Era. From that time, many of the things predicted for the messianic age would start to happen. Disease would diminish. People would live longer. Life would become easier, as the ancient curse of Adam—which condemns us not to hell, but to hard labor and painful childbirth—began to lift from humanity.

Miracles? Not really. Technology. But in the end it has the same result. In 1840, about the beginning of this period, most men died before they reached 40, most often of pneumonia, or dehydration caused by intestinal disorders. If women survived these conditions, they died in childbirth. Today most people die of heart disease or cancer, both of which tend to strike a number of years after men and women in the 1840s would already be dead.

And we're making progress on these, too.

And on Monday, Rabin and Arafat stood in front of the world and shook hands. It gives you hope we're getting closer.

After demanding that Abraham be willing to give everything for his beliefs, God redeemed Isaac. In the same way he will also, one day, redeem Israel. And, through Israel, redeem all of humanity.

And it's up to us to make the conditions right.

Thinking Jewish

[September 17, 1993] The conclusion of Rosh Ha'Shanah brings to mind the use of the *rosh*, or "head." Thinking. The way we look at the world.

Not everyone will believe it, but there really is a difference between Jewish thinking and non-Jewish thinking. We look at the world from totally different angles. The non-Jew believes that the world is in horrible condition, and that it's a natural condition. Because Adam got hungry, every human being who follows him is inherently corrupt and doomed to eternal damnation.

But Jews believe that God is just. That he is as zealous in his own pursuit of justice as he demands that we be. Jews don't believe in original sin because we know that it is contrary to divine law. Doesn't the Torah teach that we shall not punish the father for the sins of the child, nor the child for the sins of the father? Didn't God himself declare that he would punish the offspring of those who hate him no further than the fourth generation (and then only if they persist in the same sins), but that he would reward the descendants of the righteous to the thousandth generation? In the process, no doubt, canceling out many of the punishments earned in those subsequent generations.

Jews think one way, gentiles think a different way.

But there's a problem creeping in. More and more, Jews are adopting non-Jewish thought processes. Consider... What do you say if you step off a curb, and a car comes whizzing around the corner and almost runs you down?

Do you shout, *"Oy! Gevalt!"*

Or do you yell the name of a confused Jewish carpenter our neighbors somehow decided was God?

What do you call tomorrow? Is it *shabbos?* Or is it just Saturday?

What's the difference? Profound.

There is nothing sacred about Saturday. The people who gave it that name, and who continue to call it that, think of it as just another work day. Nothing special, except that, these days, not as many of them still have to work, But, again, this isn't because they have suddenly recognized the sanctity of the day, but only because they've decided that they need an extra day to stay home from work and mow the lawn.

But *shabbos* is different. When God created the world, he finished up on Friday afternoon and rested on *shabbos*. The name itself comes from a verb meaning "to rest," or "to cease from labor."

When the Torah tells us to observe *shabbos*, it demands that not only should *we* rest, but also everyone and everything in our household. Slaves were to be given the day off, and animals were not to be worked. Cows could be milked, because doing so may be considered a kindness to the animal, but the milk was not to be used. Horses were not to be ridden, nor oxen yoked.

Instead, the entire household would gather for *shabbos* supper, with the mother lighting the candles, and the father blessing the children, reading *Eishes Chayil* in honor of his wife, and chanting *kiddush* and *motzi*. The family table was to become like a family altar. The ordinary world would simply not intrude.

Herman Wouk, in his wonderful book, *This is my God*, writes of his own experience with *shabbos*. He tells of being in the throes of creation, trying to pull together a play that seems to be going nowhere. There is always the temptation, when the sun vanishes on Friday, to keep working.

But he doesn't. He puts aside his typewriter, and his pens, and all the things that have to do with working. Being an Orthodox Jew, he scrupulously keeps *shabbos* and, when it's over, he goes back to work brighter, sharper, and far better able to do things right.

God, in his wisdom, knew that human beings require rest. So he declared that we should do so, one day each week. And he declared that the land of Israel itself should rest one year in each seven. This year, in fact.

But if we think of *shabbos* as merely Saturday, are we going to rest? Some of our neighbors will tell us it's silly to refuse to drive a car one day a week. They will tell us it's foolish to insist on a special diet. They will tell us, in short, that it's foolish and silly to think like Jews. They'll stop short of telling us it's foolish to even *be* Jews, but that's what they believe.

And, in all honesty, too often we adopt their form of thinking. There's an old saying, which was applied whenever a Jew thought of doing something *too* Jewish? "What will the *goyim* think?" In the context of Jewish concerns, it goes back to the time of the Exodus, when Moses asked that very question of God, after he had threatened to destroy Israel and start over again with Moses and his family.

But that's not how most people have applied it in the last few centuries. We didn't raise fears of what the *goyim* would think if we did something that might reflect poorly on the Jewish people as a whole. Mostly because we tried very hard to avoid that sort of thing.

But we did ask what they'd think if we started acting like Jews. If we rather loudly declared, for instance, that we knew perfectly well what the Messiah was supposed to accomplish, and what he was supposed to be like, and their candidate was a total flop.

Well, they'd be upset, sure. It's hard to accept that you've been deluding yourself for nearly two millennia. But people believed that rotting meat spontaneously generated maggots for far longer than that, and that was never true, and no one seemed to be bothered when they found out the truth.

The most recent poll tells us that 52% of Jews today are marrying out. More than half. The figures are slightly alarmist, granted, as they indicate the number of spouses who weren't *born* Jewish, and not the percentage at the time of the wedding. But even allowing rather generously for conversions, it's a frightening trend. It's as if we've decided to marry ourselves right out of existence.

And how do we fight this trend? Again, it goes back to thinking like Jews. To making our Jewishness so deep a part of ourselves that intermarriage becomes impossible. If our Jewishness is only a thin veneer over an assimilated soul, it hardly matters who we marry. But, if we are truly Jewish, right down to the core, then intermarriage ceases to be an option.

Duties to Holocaust victims, or appeals to non-assimilated ancestors, or the surprising objections of parents we thought didn't even care—none of these are as compelling as the simple realization that we could never be really happy with someone who didn't share what is most central to our existence.

We have to learn—or re-learn—to think as Jews. If we don't, we will eventually vanish.

www.ingramcontent.com/pod-product-compliance
Lightning Source LLC
Chambersburg PA
CBHW030002050426
42451CB00006B/91